Chaney's Ba[...]

Lon Jr., The Wolf Man, 1[...]

A Biographic[...]

Bill Fleck

Just Pay the Ransom Music

Copyright © 2021, William J. Fleck. All rights reserved.

Published by Just Pay the Ransom Music, Wurtsboro NY.

All rights reserved. No part of this publication may be reproduced, distributed, or transmitted in any form or by any means, including photocopying, recording, or other electronic or mechanical methods, without prior written permission of the publisher, except in the case of brief quotations embodied in critical reviews and certain other noncommercial uses permitted by copyright law. For permission requests, write to the publisher, addressed "Attention: Permissions Coordinator," at the address below.

Just Pay the Ransom Music
1109 Wurtsboro Mountain Road
Wurtsboro NY 12790

www.justpaytheransommusic.org

Ordering information:

Quantity sales. Special discounts may be available on quantity purchases by corporations, associations, and others. For details, contact the publisher at the address above.

Although the author and publisher have made every effort to ensure that the information in this book was correct at press time, the author and publisher do not assume and hereby disclaim any liability to any party for any loss, damage, or disruption caused by errors or omissions, whether such errors or omissions result from negligence, accident, or any other cause.

Cover illustrations by Kim M. Simons, copyright © 2018 by Kame Arts (kame4@hotmail.com)

Cover design by Kim M. Simons.

Fleck, Bill. 2021
    Chaney's Baby: Lon Jr., The Wolf Man, 1948, and the End of a Quest/Bill Fleck

ISBN: 9798450666204

1. Fleck, Bill. 1962 - 2. Chaney, Lon Jr. (actor)—United States--Biographical Essay

For my dad, John R. Fleck, Jr. (1929-2019), who woke my brother and me up in the middle of the night to watch Universal monster movies on TV.

Bill Fleck will donate 15% of any profits made from this book to the No Kid Hungry organization.

Readers are encouraged to support this charity, which is endorsed by Jeff Bridges:

Share Our Strength
1030 15th Street, NW
Suite 1100 W
Washington DC 20005

www.nokidhungry.org

(800) 969-4767

info@strength.org

Author's Note

What follows is an attempt to chronicle a pivotal time in the life of actor Lon Chaney, Jr., best known today for his portrayal of Larry Talbot—The Wolf Man—in classic Universal monster movies from the 1940's. This is not meant to be a comprehensive biography, though there are certainly a number of biographical elements. Rather, it is an informed piece by a longtime fan attempting to analyze a watershed moment in Chaney's life: his nearly-successful suicide attempt in April of 1948. Why would one of the more talented, prosperous people who ever lived want to kill himself—and at such a young age? I hope to answer that question. My contention is that a definite line can be drawn in Chaney's life between everything that happened before and everything that happened after.

Where individuals are directly quoted, the reader can be sure that there is a specific source—an email, a book, a website, a podcast, an interview, an article. Where individuals are paraphrased, the gist of the quote is grounded in a similarly valid source.

Where thoughts, conclusions, feelings, and/or musings are exhibited, they are drawn from the persons themselves and/or friends and colleagues familiar with them. Guesswork has been avoided unless absolutely necessary—and is plainly defined as such within the text.

Any mistakes are obviously mine, though exhaustive attempts have been made to verify every word of what you are about to read.

Bill Fleck
June 26, 2021
New York

Table of Contents

April 22, 1948………1

April 30, 1913……….9

January 5, 1935…....19

August 28, 1930……32

February 10, 1932…38

October 31, 1933…....47

June 25, 1936……….54

October 27, 1941……71

August 17, 1944……107

February 5, 1948…..136

Epilogue………….....154

Acknowledgements…162

Notes……………….....168

Sources……………….187

Index……………….....210

April 22, 1948

It's a foggy Thursday night in North Hollywood. The headlines in *Valley Times*—the local paper—are almost all bad:

Strike of 13,800 Ties Boeing's Aircraft Plant.
Motive Sought in Wife Slaying.
8 Injured in Traffic Mishaps.

Early in the evening, actor Lon Chaney Jr. stumbles into his 18-room San Fernando home.

"I've just taken 40 sleeping tablets," he announces to his wife and son.

Then he disappears.

Chaney's 36-year-old wife Patsy—formerly Patricia Beck—scrambles to call for help.

Chaney's son Ron, 18—the younger of two sons Chaney has from his first marriage—chases after him.

Ron finds his father in the garage, unconscious and crumpled on the floor of his truck.

When the cavalry arrives, things look grim. Chaney is rushed to Van Nuys hospital.

Responding police officers W.D. Goldsberry and A.J. Drobatz take Ron aside.

What happened here?

Well, Patsy and his father had a family argument, Ron says. They've been fighting a lot lately.

"Attempted suicide," Drobatz concludes in his report.

Following emergency oxygen treatments at Van Nuys, Chaney is transferred quickly to St. Joseph's in Burbank.

He's near death.

* * *

Chaney, born Creighton Tull Chaney in Oklahoma City, has recently turned 42. He's the only child of Leonidas Frank ("Lon") Chaney, a wildly successful Hollywood actor best remembered at this writing for his ability to portray grotesques with sympathy and flair.

In fact, Lon Jr.'s home (located at 12750 Hortense Street) is less than five miles from Universal Studios, where his father had starred in two of his most famous films: *The Hunchback of Notre Dame* (1923) and *The Phantom of the Opera* (1925).

Lon Jr. has managed to carve out a career in the movies himself. But he didn't dare try while his famous father lived—Pop wouldn't hear of it. It takes Chaney, Sr.'s untimely death on August 26, 1930 to get his son in the game.

But success certainly doesn't come overnight. Young Creighton tries hard for three years under his own name and basically can't get arrested. A bad divorce from Ron's mother Dorothy—now 42 herself, and well on her way to becoming president of her family's gigantic water heater business—doesn't help.

By 1935, Creighton gives in to conventional wisdom and changes his name to Lon Chaney, Jr.

"They starved me into it," he complains to anyone who'll listen.

It doesn't help. Chaney and Patsy—who get hitched in Colton, California on October 1, 1937—experience very hard times.

Lady Luck finally smiles in 1939 when Chaney gets the part of Lennie Small in director Lewis Milestone's film version of John Steinbeck's *Of Mice and Men*. He's heartbreaking in the part, and though the film doesn't make much money, it does garner an Oscar nomination for Best Picture.

As a result, Chaney gets constant offers to play big, dumb guys. The money is nice at first, but being typecast at the age of 32 doesn't sit well with him.

Then, Universal reaches out. Maybe Chaney Jr. can cash in on his name and make everyone a few bucks in a second wave of horror films? His initial contract pays him $500 smackers a week—a bit shy of $9000 at this writing when adjusted for inflation.

The plan works, at least at first. Chaney's biggest success is as Larry Talbot—The Wolf Man—in 1941. It's the only chance that Chaney is given at Universal to truly create an original character, and he is excellent in the part.

But *The Wolf Man* is an anomaly. Universal exploits Chaney by casting him in a series of retreads, forcing him to play parts made famous by others—including the Frankenstein Monster, The Mummy, and Count Dracula. The box office results are generally decent—particularly because production budgets are low—but the artistic qualities are decidedly mixed.

Then, there's Chaney's drinking.

Hollywood is never at a loss for alcoholics. But Chaney has been battling a drinking problem since his twenties. It's no secret that he's not carrying around iced tea in that flask on the set as he claims.

Eventually, word circulates: get what you can out of Chaney before early afternoon because after that, he's often smashed.

By 1945, Chaney is not a happy guy. True, he's reprised The Wolf Man role three more times—in increasingly silly potboilers, with diminishing returns—but he isn't offered parts he likes and is often miscast in those he's given.

Chaney isn't quiet about any of this.

The end of World War II temporarily kills horror films. And 1946 brings regime change to Universal. The studio—on its way to becoming Universal-International—drops Chaney from the roster.

Chaney scrambles for work. He plays big, dumb guys in films opposite comics like Bob Hope. And he plays big, dumb guys in theater reprisals of *Born Yesterday* and *Of Mice and Men*.

On Thursday, February 5, 1948, Chaney—five days shy of his birthday—returns to Universal for the first time in two years. The purpose? To play The Wolf Man in a one-off called *The Brain of Frankenstein*

The film is set for release on June 15 as *Bud Abbott and Lou Costello Meet Frankenstein*.

But it doesn't look like Chaney is going to live to see it.

* * *

The medical team at St. Joseph's works on Chaney. During the night, he wakes up briefly, and recognizes Patsy. He's put in an oxygen tent to ward off pneumonia. By early morning, doctors upgrade his status: dangerous.

By now, Chaney's oldest son—Lon Ralph, 19—has joined his brother and stepmother at the hospital.

And so has the Press. This can be risky.

One of the most important things Chaney Jr. has ever learned from his father is the importance of keeping personal issues private—especially from the newspapers.

"Between pictures, there is no Lon Chaney," Pop often told inquisitive writers.

Patsy and her husband try to live the same way. So when cornered by reporters, Patsy attempts to walk back her stepson's story regarding an argument.

"Everything was fine between us," she says. "I don't know what happened."

Lester Salkow—Chaney's agent—shows up as well.

Salkow is barely 30 years old, but he's show-biz savvy—he started acting in his teens under the name Lester Arnold. During the war, he'd served with the Army Air Forces in Okinawa, and was discharged in 1946 with the rank of First Lieutenant.[1] He and his brother Irving run The Salkow Theatrical Agency on Sunset.

Salkow knows that the general public's understanding of mental health issues—including depression—is far from enlightened. In 1948, an actor's suicide attempt can be career suicide as well. Chaney—with no studio contract—is already subject to the fickle whims of the freelance market. He doesn't need the burden of being labeled a mental case as well.

So today, Salkow knows he has to do some damage control.

"I had an appointment with Chaney this morning," he says, attempting to smooth things over. "Last night I saw him and Chaney said, 'I guess I better get to bed early. I want to have a clear head when I talk over this proposition.' It was a new film role he had been offered."

Salkow adds that Chaney was in perfectly good humor, and that his financial condition is "excellent."

This whole affair must have been an accident, Salkow concludes.

Barry Woodmansee—Chaney's attorney—is also on the scene.

This isn't Woodmansee's first rodeo. In 1943, for example, he'd represented Joan Berry—a 22-year-old actress—in a paternity suit against none other than Charlie Chaplin.[2] Woodmansee knows bad press about family problems isn't good for an actor. He makes sure Patsy reinforces the party line.

"It's ridiculous even to think he would want to destroy himself," she tells the press. "He had so much to live for."

"He was not trying to commit suicide," Woodmansee reiterates. "He had not been arguing with his wife." Rather, Woodmansee claims, Chaney had been feeling "overworked" and took the pills for a good night's sleep.

"I'm handling details for construction of a summer home at Lake Tahoe for them," Woodmansee declares. "That doesn't seem to indicate marital troubles."

Though still in a semi-coma, Chaney's condition goes from "just fair" to "improving."

Meanwhile, Universal suits are quick to report that they doubt "his constant portrayal of grisly roles depressed him," though they say he seemed "very preoccupied" while shooting *Abbott and Costello Meet Frankenstein*.

* * *

Monday, April 26. Chaney is reported as "much improved." By Wednesday, he recovers enough to go home.

On Tuesday, May 11, reporter Ruth Brigham makes this unkind observation in print:

"When Lon Chaney Jr. recently overdosed himself, it made big black headlines. The next day, a minor bit player rated two paragraphs from the police records."

Of course, the incident eventually fades from the public consciousness. Chaney soldiers on, and everything appears to be back to normal.

Nothing to see here, folks.

Today, Chaney's suicide attempt is treated like a footnote.[3] Fans of the actor are often surprised to learn that he made an attempt at all—especially in the wake of having just reprised his beloved Wolf Man in what has become a classic film. Why would one of the more successful people who ever walked the planet want to kill himself? And at such a young age?

The answer lies in everything that has gone on up until the moment before he swallows those pills.

April 30, 1913

Cleva Creighton Chaney watches her husband from the wings of the 1600-seat Majestic Theatre in Los Angeles. He's frolicking on stage dressed as a clown.

As he acknowledges the applause and exits the stage, Cleva catches his eye.

Then she swallows a vial of bichloride of mercury and crumbles at his feet.

Cleva is 23. Of Irish ancestry, she's tall and thin with dark hair, blue eyes, and a beautiful singing voice. She's a popular cabaret singer who is expected to drink with clients after the show, which she does—to her husband's ever-increasing exasperation.

They have a 7-year-old son named Creighton.

* * *

Cleva is born Frances Cleveland Creighton on August 20, 1889 in Kansas. Her father John is a drunk who ditches his wife and four kids. Her mother Martha—commonly known as Mattie—supports the family by working as a practical nurse, a cook, and a washerwoman.

By the time she's 15, Cleva is working the switchboard at the phone company in Oklahoma City. It's there that a girlfriend shows her an ad in the local paper:

The Columbia Musical Comedy Repertoire Company is looking for chorus girls.

"You ought to try out for that, Cleva," the girlfriend says. "Gee, with a voice like yours! Look what you might do—get to be an actress."

Mattie, however, is dead set against the idea.

"You stay away from there," she tells her daughter. "I don't hold with girls going on the stage. It's not your class. You've got a good job. Stay where you are."

The next day, however, Cleva manages to convince her mother to at least let her audition.

At the theater, a young man emerges from behind the scenery. He's wearing a sweater and overalls. A cigarette burns in his mouth. He looks Cleva up and down.

"Nope," he says.

He's Lon Chaney. Among the many jobs he does for the company is recruiting local talent. It makes sense—you can't travel the theater circuit profitably hauling a large group of dancers around, but local folks are bound to spend a few bucks to see their relatives on stage.

Chaney is a dancer himself—a good one. Born in Colorado Springs on April Fool's Day in 1883, he's just shy of 22. But he's seen a few things.

To begin with, both his parents are deaf-mute.

Frank Chaney and Emma Kennedy met at a school for the mute—established by Emma's father—and married late in 1877. Frank made his living as a barber. Lon has an older brother named Jonathan, a younger sister named Caroline, and a baby brother named George.[1] His parents raised him on a gospel of hard work and self-reliance. Weakness was shunned.

Illness confines Emma to bed early in Lon's life. He foregoes school to help care for her and develops a penchant for pantomime—a skill that will eventually make him his fortune. His older brother manages a theater, and it's there that Lon gets his start in 1902.

Now he's in Oklahoma City looking Cleva over. And he instinctively knows she can't dance.

He turns to go back to work.

"Maybe you'd like to hear me sing?" Cleva tries.

"Sure," he smiles, "but I'm awful busy this morning."

"I *can* sing," Cleva insists.

It's obvious that she isn't going away.

"Shoot," Chaney says with a laugh.

She launches into a number, a cappella. Yeah, she can sing. And how!

"You're hired," he says.

Cleva is thrilled. Not only does she have a job in the theater, but she's also smitten with her new boss.

Lon Chaney in 1905 is ruggedly attractive. He's five-seven and 150 pounds, with dark hair parted in the middle and a strong jaw. Most impressive are his expressive brown eyes, set under thick brows. Plus, he has a quick sense of humor and a boatload of talent.

Over the next few days, he tries to teach Cleva to dance, but this proves to be impossible. Instead, he finds ways to utilize her magnificent voice on stage.

And he falls in love with her.

As a result of his puritanical upbringing, many of the characteristics Chaney decidedly manifests in full adulthood have already taken root in him: His code of ethics. His attention to detail. His desire for privacy. His strict ideas about loyalty. His love of the outdoors, the company of close friends, and the sharing of a few drinks.

Romantic love is something new to him.

Lon Chaney is not a trusting person. But he trusts Cleva Creighton and gives her his heart. She reciprocates.

They have a whirlwind summer.

But late in the fall, Cleva has something she needs to tell him.

She's pregnant.[2]

Neither Cleva nor Lon is ready for this. Both are just starting their careers—how are they ever going to manage with a kid?

Panic overtakes them. Things get tense. Cleva will say in later years that Lon even suggests that she should get an abortion.

Instead, they decide they need stability. They claim to be married.[3] In December, they return to Oklahoma City so Cleva's mother can help out.

Needless to say, Mattie is in full "I-told-you-so" mode when she hears the news. In her mind, Chaney's behavior has reinforced everything she believes about theatrical folks being immoral.

For his part, Chaney gets a job in a furniture store owned by a family named Tull. He's paid $15 a week—about $425 when adjusted for inflation at this writing.

Though Lon's initial displeasure regarding the pregnancy has worried her—Cleva knows he has the memory of an elephant, and fears he may one day resent her—she's grateful to find that he's very sweet and supportive during the months before she delivers. And she needs that care and support because her pregnancy is a rough one. Her discomfort is constant, and she spends nearly all of her time in bed.

* * *

Saturday, February 10, 1906. Cleva prematurely delivers a son. Initially, the baby suffers from lack of oxygen, but rallies.[4] They name him Creighton Tull Chaney—Creighton after his mom, and Tull after Lon's generous boss at the furniture store.

* * *

Thursday, May 31, 1906. Lon and Cleva quietly—but finally officially—marry. In later years, they will try to cover up their unwed status at the time of Creighton's birth.

With renewed enthusiasm, the Chaneys decide that life on the road working in the theater has to be superior to raising their son in Oklahoma City, especially since Mattie isn't warming up to Lon.

But once on the circuit, money is a constant issue. Bookings evaporate if ticket sales lag. The Chaneys stash every cent they can as a bulwark against unemployment. Lon will be obsessive about money for the rest of his life.

Things between them begin to fall apart when Cleva initially proves to be the more popular performer. This, of course, is not hard to understand. Cleva is attractive and a great singer. When business is slow for the comedy troupe, she's able to pick up gigs in cabarets. She puts on a show for sure, and is expected to drink with the clientele—mostly male—afterward, which she's happy to do.

Slowly, the teetotaling girl who took Lon Chaney's heart in 1905 is developing a drinking problem.

Then, too, jealousy enters the picture. Chaney—working like a maniac, trying to set his career on fire—is not the most attentive of husbands.

Cleva *craves* attention.

She often finds solace talking with bartenders. When Chaney realizes that his wife is treating other men as confidants, he goes ballistic. Is she cheating on him?

"Don't be too hard on Cleva," Lon's brother John advises.

But the jealousy cuts both ways—Cleva is angered herself when she perceives that pretty showgirls are flirting with her man.

By 1912, Cleva is billing herself as *Cleva Creighton* rather than *Cleva Chaney*.

Cleva and Lon aren't alone in their pain. Their son Creighton is affected, too. Yes, he is clothed and fed, but his folks are often too busy to spend time with him, and he's pawned off on company players—Hazel

Hastings and Fay Parkes in particular. As of 1912, Creighton has yet to attend school.

Sadly, when Lon spends time with his son it's often because Cleva is too drunk to take care of him herself.

"I guess I was just a woman who shouldn't ever have taken a drink," Cleva will say years later.

Things reach a breaking point when Chaney—doubling as stage manager at The Majestic—plans to hit the road with the Kolb and Dill Company when they leave California.

Cleva is not happy about the idea. She and Lon clash—hard.

Cleva becomes frantic. After her show at the Brink's Café, she heads to the Majestic Theatre and tries to persuade her husband one last time.

But Lon is unmoved.

And so Cleva stands in the wings, catches Lon's eye, and downs the poison.

* * *

She's rushed to the hospital in an ambulance. Lon—still dressed as a clown—rides with her.

Bichloride of mercury is bad stuff. Not only is mercury deadly; the substance is corrosive. Surviving a dose like Cleva has taken is unlikely.

But at the hospital, police surgeons treat her with antidotes. When she regains consciousness, they ask her what happened.

"I quarreled with my husband," Cleva says, "and life had lost its brightness."

She begs throughout the night to see her son.

* * *

Thursday, May 1, 1913. Cleva's doctor takes Lon aside.

"She'll live," he says, "but she'll be a sick girl for a long time."

Like Patsy Chaney 35 years later, Lon's first thought is damage control.

"It's true we quarreled," he tells *The Los Angeles Herald*, "but my wife had no intention of attempting suicide. She believed she was swallowing medicine. Our differences are all straightened out now."

Of course, none of this is true—Cleva was very much trying to kill herself, as she admits to *The Los Angeles Daily Times* that very same day. But Chaney needs people to *think* he's telling the truth.

And as for their differences being straightened out?

By May 26, the Chaneys are separated.

Creighton spends some time with his mom after her release from the hospital—at first.

But then, Chaney comes across a yet-to-be mailed letter Cleva has written to Don A. Traeger, one of her bartender friends:

> "My dearest boy: Received your letters and will take a few lines before I go to breakfast. Creighton is in the bathtub and I am in my nightgown. I sent you a letter about three days ago and gave it to a girl to mail. Did you get it? I told you that I was working at Clunes, 5th and Main. Gee, honey, you don't know how sick I am of work. I don't know what is the matter with me. The doctor says I have lost control of my nerves. I am taking medicine all the time. Say dearie I hope you can come here within two weeks as it will be much easier for me to see you while I am at Clunes. Well Don I must close and wash the baby.[5] Yours all the time with love, Cleva."

Confronted, Cleva admits to being in love with Traeger. She's also expecting money from him. She says she's done with Lon.

For Chaney—whose motto might as well be, "When I'm through I'm through, and when I'm through, I'm *all* through"—this is proof-positive that Cleva needs to be cut out of his life.

He will never trust her again—in any capacity.

Attempting to build a slam-dunk divorce case, Chaney begins spying on his estranged wife. In addition to being involved with Traeger, he determines that she has been shacking up with Charles Osmand, another bartender.

Lon Chaney is going to make her pay.

But he's going to wound his son deeply in the process.

* * *

December 13, 1913. Lon Chaney files for divorce from Cleva Creighton. He petitions for sole custody of his son.

Not only will Cleva no longer be his wife.

She will not be Creighton's mother, either.

But how will he explain her absence to the child?

January 5, 1935

The headline on page 11 of *The Indianapolis Star* reads, "Lon Chaney's Son Plans to Assume Name for Screen."

"I am not interested in using my father's name in order to make a lot of money," the actor says. "If I'd wanted that, I could have cashed in heavily when I began, and then quit. But I am interested in making a real success in pictures, and my ambition is to make something out of myself in them. I believe that as 'Lon Chaney Jr.,' I can get the opportunity to do so that is denied to Creighton Chaney."

It's a noble sentiment that contains a great deal of truth.

But for Creighton Chaney, it's also an admission of crushing defeat.

* * *

Wednesday, April 1, 1914. Creighton's father Lon turns 31.

He's also in court attempting to divorce Cleva.

His charges are devastating. Adultery. Habitual intemperance. The infliction of mental anguish on her husband.

Cleva is a no-show.

A letter to her estranged husband is entered for the court's consideration:

"Don't think I am going to ask for forgiveness. I want permission to see our boy. I have paid and am still paying dearly for it. But you don't care and I can't expect even a word from you; but for God's sake grant my only hold to the name of Chaney, and let me see my dear baby. I would be a slave or anything else just to see him. I promise I will not beg your forgiveness or harm you in any way. I know, Lon, that you loved me once, and to think I am not worthy of that love. Lon, I am almost crazy. Please return good for evil once more as you have always done with me."

The next day, the judge returns his decision. The bans of marriage will be dissolved in one year's time, and Chaney will have "care, custody and control" of Creighton.

There is a proviso: "[B]ut that defendant be permitted to see said child at all reasonable times, provided that defendant not be under the influence of liquor, and that she conduct herself in a proper manner."

There is no chance in Hell that Lon Chaney is going to allow this in any way, shape, or form.

"What could I do?" Cleva will say in 1950. "I didn't have a penny. I didn't know where Lon and the boy were. The stuff I'd taken did something to my vocal cords. When I tried to get a job, I opened my mouth and couldn't sing a note. Lon didn't know about that."

Chaney isn't exactly living large, either.

To begin with, the scandal surrounding Cleva's suicide and their divorce costs him his job with Kolb and Dill.

Then, on April 8, a heart attack kills his mother.

Finally, he's hustling so much that his sister Carrie has to take care of 8-year-old Creighton.

Something has to give.

In what turns out to be a fortuitous decision, Chaney decides to give motion pictures a try. He puts Creighton in a home for children of divorce and disaster while attempting to make some money. He visits the boy on Sundays.

He also tells Creighton that Cleva is dead.

In so doing, what exactly is Lon Chaney thinking? Sure, she's dead to *him*, so this may be a beneficial—though selfish—fantasy. But it's devastating for Creighton. The vulnerable boy feels abandoned by his mother's 'death.' A distrust of women begins to grow in him.

And how will Lon ever explain this to Creighton if and when the kid finds out he's been lied to about something so crucial?

Lon Chaney has weaved a tangled web.

* * *

Friday, November 26, 1915. The courthouse in Santa Ana, California. Lon Chaney and Hazel Hastings get hitched.

Born Marie Genevieve Hazel Bennett in San Francisco, the 28-year-old Hazel is a former dancer. Catholic, and Italian on her mother's side, she's tiny—standing only 4'10"—but very smart.

The match is a good one. Like Chaney, Hazel is a veteran of a bad first marriage—hers was to Charles Stuart Hastings, who sells cigars and is severely handicapped.[1] She and Chaney also share an ability to immediately—and accurately—size up people and situations. As the years go on, they will very much be partners in both business and life.

Oh, and Chaney will tell everyone that Hazel is Creighton's mother.

By the time they get 9-year-old Creighton out of boarding school and bring him home—1607 Edgemont Avenue, Los Angeles—Chaney is making $45 a week over at Universal, worth a little more than $1100 at this writing when adjusted for inflation. As time goes on, this is raised to $60, then to $75.

But the always shrewd Hazel thinks her husband is being cheated. She knows what his talent is worth.

"You will ask for $150 a week from now on," she tells him. "There are not many in the movies with your stage experience…A man must never settle for less than he is worth."

Chaney balks, at first. But he eventually makes the demand…and gets it.

Still, no matter how rich and famous Chaney gets—and he gets *very* rich and famous—two things remain constant:

There will be no mention of Cleva. Ever.

And Creighton will not be coddled.[2]

"He's no rich man's son," Chaney says. "He'll earn what he gets, the same as I did."

* * *

Tuesday, April 1, 1919. Lon Chaney turns 36.

That same day, a small announcement appears on page 8 in the *Visalia Times-Delta*:

> **Licensed to Wed.** William Bush, age 43, native of California, resident of San Diego, and Oleva [*sic*] Creighton Chaney, age 29, native of Kansas, resident of Ogden, Utah.

If anyone in the Chaney household is aware of this, no one says anything about it.

* * *

True to his word, Chaney is not raising Creighton like a rich man's son.

Beginning at age 14, Creighton is expected to have a job after school and every summer. He works in slaughter houses and butcher shops. He picks apricots. He also tries out for Hollywood High's football team, but is cut—though he's already six feet tall, he's a string bean at 125 pounds.

During his junior year, he meets a pretty, red-headed, 12-year-old girl named Patricia Beck and teaches her how to play tennis. She's a pupil at Los Feliz Grammar School.

She will eventually become his second wife.

Like his father, Creighton nurtures a lifelong love of animals and nature. The family's favorite outdoor spot is near Big Pine in the Sierra Nevada Mountains. The hunting and fishing are excellent there. In 1929, Chaney has a beautiful stone cabin built. Many of Creighton's most cherished memories stem from these outings.

But he doesn't like school much.

"Regular schooling wasn't for me," he'll say years later. "I liked getting around. I never remember not working."

The fact that he's often bullied on campus doesn't help.

At one point—after appearing in small parts in school plays—he asks his father about maybe making a few bucks as an extra in films, something some of the other kids do on the weekends.

Lon Chaney will not hear of it.

"Dad never seemed like a star or an actor to me," Creighton explains. "He had a curious suspicion of his newfound success. He always doubted it, always feared it would end. He kept up his membership in the stagehand's union to his dying day, just in case."[3]

Chaney thinks Creighton should be a bank teller or maybe a plumber. Every time the possibility of an acting career for his son is mentioned, Chaney washes it away in freezing cold water.

"He's 6'2" tall," Chaney says as late as 1928. "That's too tall.[4] He'd have to have parts built around him."

Underneath it all, however, something more sinister lurks—something Chaney sees whenever he catches his son's sad, hazel eyes.

He sees Cleva.

Like Cleva, Creighton is overly sensitive. He requires attention. He has self-esteem issues. Criticism cuts him deeply.

In today's world, we'd say that both Creighton and his mother are bipolar.

Growing up in the wings of the theater, being passed around to various relatives and friends, and residing in foster homes and boarding schools before finally entering a stable phase at the age of nine has crippled Creighton emotionally. Who can he believe in? And how does he know?

Chaney understands how hard it is to make it in The Biz. He doesn't trust his own success, and he describes himself as "hard-boiled." How would the inevitable career knocks affect his son, who is soft like his mother? Creighton won't even stand up to bullies in school—how will he ever be able to handle Hollywood? Might he—like Cleva—maybe even contemplate suicide?

"I just don't want my son in this business," he'll confide in a friend.[5] "Maybe he'd survive. Most of them don't. It's a crazy racket. You know that. I'd been through hell and back before I got into it, so it didn't upset me much. Besides, I could afford to stay away from most of it. The kid's different. I want to keep him out of Hollywood. I'm not afraid he'd be a failure. I'm afraid he'd be a success. I'd rather he'd be a good plumber than a movie star."

In short, Chaney believes failure would damage his son. And success would kill him.

Creighton, for his part, understands his father's stature in motion pictures.

"I wouldn't want to go into pictures on your name," he tells Pop. "If I could use another name—and top you—I'd give it a fling. But nobody's ever going to top you."

Then, too, he loves his father and has been taught to be obedient.

"I wouldn't for the world have done anything Dad didn't want me to do," he'll say later.

Sadly, Lon Chaney thinks he's giving Creighton the lessons he needs to overcome his growing demons. But deep down, Lon's tough-love approach confuses his son. Like Cleva before him, Creighton finds Lon's aloofness—in the attempt to make a man out of him—disturbing. Plus, he senses his father's reservations about him.

The idea that Pop thinks he isn't tough devastates him, causing him to worry about his masculinity.

And then John Jeske enters the mix.

* * *

Born in Skierniewice, Poland on May 7, 1890 to a Polish mother and a German father, the 30-year-old Jeske has been in the United States since 1912. Initially, he works at his brother's bakery in Scranton, PA, but by 1914, he's living in Los Angeles. He works as an auto mechanic and applies for U.S. citizenship in 1920.

By 1923, he's just started duties at Louis Mansey's garage near Hollywood when Lon Chaney—a regular customer, and a friend of Mansey's—pulls in.

Who's the new guy? Chaney asks the owner. Mansey introduces them.

Chaney and Jeske—who resembles Chaney enough to be mistaken for his brother—hit it off. Before long, Jeske is officially hired as the Chaney family's chauffeur.

Unofficially, Jeske quietly helps Lon with his makeup and costumes—"unofficially" because all the publicity says that Lon Chaney does everything himself.

Jeske's first assignment? *The Hunchback of Notre Dame.*

Behind closed doors—following Chaney's instructions, of course—Jeske helps work up and apply the materials necessary to turn Lon into Quasimodo.

Before long, Jeske becomes a staple at the Chaney home as well. This does not sit right with Creighton.

Now a junior in high school, Creighton—who has an inherent dislike of people he perceives to be "foreigners"—is suspicious of Jeske because he's German. This is odd, given his father's broadminded view on such matters.

When Jeske begins spending more and more time with his beloved Pop, Creighton's aversion becomes definite dislike.

Why isn't Dad spending his time with *me*?

Eventually—as we will see—it becomes full-blown hate.

Not surprisingly, Creighton makes a dramatic bid for Pop's attention when he decides he needs to stop the bullying he's been experiencing in school once and for all. To that end, he seeks out his primary antagonist.....and beats the guy to a pulp.

Then, he makes a list of every other kid who's done him wrong, and thrashes them one at a time as well.

As a result, he's kicked out of school.

For his part, Lon is encouraged by the fact that Creighton has finally shown some guts. But the kid has to finish his education somewhere, so Chaney has him take courses at the Disabled American Veteran's Institute. Six months later, Creighton comes out with a certificate in business.

With college out of the question—"The Chaneys don't run to that sort of thing," Lon decrees—Creighton ends up working as a boiler maker at what will become the General Water Heater Corporation in Los Angeles.

It's there that he meets his first wife.

* * *

Dorothy M. Hinckley is born October 30, 1905 in Colorado. By 1920, her parents—Ralph and Emma (formerly Metzger)—have moved the family to Los Angeles, where Ralph begins making and selling water heaters out of his hardware store.

His company will eventually make one out of every seven water heaters sold on the west coast.

The Hinckleys are real society; their get-togethers are reported regularly by local newspapers. And the dark-haired Dorothy is as shrewd as Hazel Chaney. By 1927, she will be elected to the board of directors of her father's company.

By 1927, she's also already married to Creighton.

When Dorothy meets him, Creighton—now 20—is taller than most guys, with his father's eyebrows and prominent nose, and his mother's soft chin. A few years of physical labor have filled him out and muscled him up. With his thick brown hair and hazel eyes, he's certainly attractive enough to turn Dorothy's head.

At first, Dorothy's father isn't sure about the young man in his daughter's life. But Creighton has a dedicated, salt-of-the-earth side to him. He's intelligent and fun to be with, plus he has the spirit of an entrepreneur. He passes all of Ralph's tests.

Sunday, April 25, 1926. Creighton—now a salesman—marries his boss's daughter. Pop and Hazel give them a house for a wedding present, while Dorothy's parents have it furnished.

Luckily, Dorothy makes a good impression on Creighton's infamously skeptical folks. Hazel—perhaps sensing a kindred spirit in Dorothy—often helps out at Emma's parties, and Lon is very complimentary about his daughter-in-law when asked about his son in 1930.

"He's happy in business and he's got a great wife," Pop crows.

The early years with Dorothy bring out the best in Creighton. His humor and charm are regularly on display, and he adapts to high society well, even serving as an usher at his brother-in-law's wedding.

Being outdoors is still a joy for him, as is attending get-togethers at his father's place. There, alcohol and stories flow, and Pop takes some of his beloved family movies with a 16mm camera.

For Creighton, it's a marvelous place to be…that is, when he's not irked by Jeske's presence.

What, exactly, does Pop see in this guy?

* * *

Tuesday, July 3, 1928. Creighton and Dorothy welcome their son, naming him Lon Ralph Chaney after their fathers.

"I'm grandpop now," Lon says. "Guess I can spoil this one. Creighton'll have to look after him. I can have some fun."

He's equally thrilled when grandson Number 2—Ronald Creighton—arrives on Tuesday, March 18, 1930.

If anything, Creighton is even more thrilled than his father. He harbors a genuine, deep, lifelong love of children.

Meanwhile, he is well on his way to becoming the secretary of Ralph Hinckley's company. He supplements his income by teaching wrestling at the Hollywood Athletic Club. When his boys are old enough, he teaches them to wrestle as well. He claims that he wrestles at least an hour a day—oftentimes more—but gives it up when Dorothy puts her foot down: stop complaining about injuries, or stop wrestling. He still enjoys tennis and golf, plus he loves to play bridge.

In short, this is a relatively calm period in Creighton's life.

But crippling disaster is about to strike.

August 28, 1930

Lon Chaney, 47, is dead.

Outside the Los Angeles funeral parlor, a large crowd has gathered spontaneously. Police are called to control them.

Inside, Hazel Chaney is screaming, "Why? Why? Why?"

Creighton attempts to comfort his stepmom, but he's at a loss as to how. It doesn't help that Jeske is one of Pop's pall bearers. A nurse takes charge of Hazel.

"Laugh, Clown, Laugh"—Chaney's favorite song from one of his favorite films—floats up from behind the flowers and fills the chapel.

* * *

Chaney's illness had been a closely-guarded secret.

It begins innocently enough when he catches a cold while shooting the film *Thunder* in April of 1929. The malady quickly develops into pneumonia.

In September of 1929, fed up with his constantly sore throat, Chaney has his tonsils out. He doesn't get any better.

In October, he's told he has lung cancer. Of course, he keeps it quiet.

"I don't want to die," he confides to his friend, writer Adela Rogers St. Johns. "I hate going into that unknown darkness. But I can lick that. I don't want to leave my wife and my son and the babies. I love them so. What will I do without Hazel? What will she do without me? I don't want to die. I'm not ready."

Sick as he is, Chaney still manages to make his one-and-only talking picture—the hit remake of his 1925 film *The Unholy Three*, for which he earns rave reviews. But Chaney is an increasingly weakening man.

While rumors swirl around Hollywood that Universal wants to cast him in the talkie version of *Dracula*, Chaney is privately coughing up blood. Things get so bad that Jeske moves in with the Chaneys to handle household tasks.

Creighton, who has yet to be told that his father is even sick, nevertheless senses that Pop might be dying. The very thought crushes him.

On June 23, 1930, Chaney makes out his Last Will and Testament.

By July, he's hemorrhaging multiple times a day.

Hospitalized at St. Vincent's on August 20, Chaney is given blood transfusions. The newspapers are told he's anemic. An MGM executive says that Chaney is "holding his own" and improving.

In reality, Chaney has lost the ability to speak. He communicates with Hazel, Creighton, and his brother John through sign language. Jeske is entrusted with handling all business at the Chaney household in his absence.

At about 12:55 on the morning of August 26, Chaney suffers a fatal hemorrhage. Creighton and Hazel are there. Chaney's doctors are powerless to save him. It's all over.

He's interred at Forest Lawn Cemetery next to his own father.

At 3 PM, all of the studios in Hollywood observe two minutes of silence in Chaney's honor. But for Creighton, the gesture is small potatoes.

"Then, Hollywood picked up its newly-acquired microphone and forgot," he'll complain bitterly.

As far as Creighton Tull Chaney knows, both of his biological parents are now dead. He feels very much alone.

* * *

September 4, 1930. Lon Chaney's estate is probated.

Chaney has left behind $550,000, worth about $8.5 million as of this writing. Hazel, as his "dear, beloved wife," receives most of it, plus $150,000 in real estate and $125,000 in personal property.

Oddly, Cleva Creighton benefits as well:

"So that there may be no misunderstanding or contest of any kind whatsoever," Chaney instructs, "I hereby give and bequeath to Cleva Creighton Bush the sum of $1 and no more. I am divorced from Cleva Creighton Bush and I am under no obligations whatever to provide anything further or additional than herein contained."

Even in death, Lon Chaney has a long memory.

As for Lon's siblings—and his son—the will instructs that $275,000 in life insurance is to be split four ways. Each share would be worth more than $4 million today.

Creighton has Dorothy put their cut away in trust for their sons.

But what gets under Creighton's skin is the fact that John Jeske—"at all times loyal to me," Pop has decreed—is awarded $5000 for himself, worth slightly less than $79,000 today.

With the Great Depression on, Creighton thinks that money should be his. Did Pop value Jeske more than he valued his own son?

His smoldering rage is ignited again when it becomes obvious that Jeske and Hazel are leaning on each other for support after Pop's death. Whose side is Hazel on?

* * *

Meanwhile, news of Chaney's will has gotten Adela Rogers St. Johns curious…

Who is Cleva Creighton Bush?

St. Johns digs into public records. She discovers what Lon Chaney never wanted anyone to remember.

He had a first wife.

And that first wife is Creighton's mother.

Creighton is already irked by the fact that Jeske has received $5000 in his father's will. He's also nursing a growing resentment of Hazel, believing that her portion of the estate is too generous. More recently, his stepmom has offended him by donating Lon's makeup kit and some costumes to the Natural History Museum in Los Angeles—items Creighton believes are rightfully his. It's as if everyone is telling him that his father really didn't care that much about him.

When Creighton finds out that Pop and Hazel had lied to him about Cleva's death, he is understandably apoplectic.[1] The implications are devastating.

What gave them the right to essentially steal his mother from him?

How can he ever trust Hazel again? Or the memory of his father?

"I always got the impression that the boy never quite forgave his father when after Lon was dead, young Creighton—known professionally as Lon, Jr.—found out about his own mother and went to see her," Adela Rogers St. John will write. "It also seemed to me he held it against his stepmother, who was always very kind to him, that Lon Chaney had left her outright every penny of his fortune to do with as she pleased."

Meanwhile, St. Johns tracks down Cleva in Pasadena.

She finds a sad but resigned 41-year-old woman, who claims to have seen her son only once since 1914: as a grown man through a window.

Even so, she declares that she is not angry.

"I never envied him his success," Cleva says about Chaney. "I never felt bitter. I used to sit in movie theaters and watch him on the screen. I was proud of him. I figured the boy was better off with him. Only I thought Lon might have let me see him, but he never answered my letters, and then I heard he was married again."

After her split from Chaney, Cleva had spent time in Utah. Returning to California, she subsisted on manual labor. She worked in beet fields in Oxnard and cooked for 50 field hands in the hot sun.

By the time St. Johns catches up with her, Cleva has been married to William Bush—now 55—for more than ten years. They work a farm, and have a 1-year-old daughter named Stella.

Just like that, Creighton has a half-sister he might never have known about had his father's lie not come to light.

Cleva tells St. Johns that she'd spent her $1 inheritance on flowers...which she claims to have scattered over Chaney's grave.

Inevitably, of course, Creighton decides to go and see his mother. Things between them are awkward at first.[2] Still smarting from his father and stepmother's deception, he also harbors a resentment toward Cleva for abandoning him. He simply can't understand why his mom wouldn't have moved mountains to be a part of his life, no matter what his father's wishes may have been.

Of course, Creighton's default position is to blame himself. Is there something wrong with him? Is he that unlovable? His distrust of women becomes worse.

Eventually—though he'll never mention her in interviews—Cleva and Creighton forge a relationship.

But Creighton Chaney's feelings for his father have changed. Before long, he'll happily defy Pop's strictest edict.

He'll become an actor.

And he'll top the bastard.

February 10, 1932

Wednesday, February 10, 1932. Creighton Chaney turns 26.[1]

He also signs his first motion picture contract with none other than David O. Selznick—the eventual mastermind behind *Gone with the Wind* (1939)—at RKO.

The contract stipulates that Chaney "will be given ample opportunity to demonstrate his ability to earn his own way as an actor."

Interestingly, it also notes that he "will be known as Creighton Chaney, and not under any circumstances as Lon Chaney, Junior." Creighton has insisted on this clause.

Initially, he'll be paid $200 a week, a bit shy of $4000 today. Given what's occurred since his father's death, the money is very welcome.

* * *

"You're Lon Chaney's son! You ought to be in pictures!"

It's 1931. Creighton—by now a secretary at his father-in-law's water heater company—is toying with the idea of acting. Though Hazel Chaney knows that her husband had been dead set against the idea, she tries to mend fences with her stepson by calling a few contacts and get-ting him invited to studio parties. Perhaps he'll be discovered?

It's at one of these parties that Creighton takes center stage and belts out a song he's written himself.

A Hollywood assistant director likes the tune.

"Why don't you take it around to our music department?" he suggests.

When Creighton does, he's greeted by a casting director and told he should be making movies.

"How 'bout it?" Creighton responds.

The casting director promises him a job "in a couple of days."

"That hit me right," Chaney will say later. "I was fed up with regularity and thought he had a good idea."

Rashly—there's a Depression on with no end in sight, after all—Chaney tells Ralph Hinckley he's done with the General Water Heater Corporation.

This sets Dorothy back on her heels. They have two little kids. The stock market crash in 1929 has hit her father's company hard—after all, water heaters are considered to be luxury items. Profits have disappeared. The 50-plus employees—each personally known to the Hinckley family—have taken a 20% cut in pay. Executives like Dorothy have to eat a 50% cut.

And her husband chooses *now* to quit his job and try acting?

Sensing disaster, Dorothy takes steps to legally lock Creighton out of their sons' trust fund.

Meanwhile, a couple of days go by, and then a couple of weeks. The studio doesn't call.

"I haven't heard from that casting office yet," an increasingly anxious Chaney jokes.

No one's laughing.

Anytime Chaney calls the casting director, he's told the man is unavailable.

Money gets tight. Dorothy has to sink precious trust fund dollars into the General Water Heater Corporation to keep the doors open. She and Creighton argue constantly.

That spring—adding gas to the fire—Adela Rogers St. Johns publishes a series of biographical pieces on Lon Chaney in *Liberty* magazine. The second installment on May 9 notes that John Jeske was a close confidant of Chaney's who could always be found in Chaney's dressing room.

Creighton is once again infuriated. *Will this damn Jeske be in his life forever?*

Hurt and in need of cash, Creighton confronts his stepmom. He demands more of his father's money. He frightens her, but she doesn't come across.

To save face, he begins telling people the lie that his father died broke.

Luckily for him, the assistant director who had gotten this acting ball rolling in the first place feels guilty. He sets up a meeting with a casting director at RKO. They do three screen tests on Chaney, sans makeup. He deliberately avoids any imitation of his father. Studio execs dub the tests "very good." Chaney hires Edward Small as his agent.

RKO offers him a five-year contract. His pay is to start at $250 a week, with gradual increases to $3500.

But he has to sign as Lon Chaney, Jr.

Creighton refuses. The execs ask him to think about it. He goes to see Hazel.

"My mother knows more about the workings and inner-workings of pictures than anybody I have ever met," he'll tell *The Hollywood Report* in 1935. "She knew why they had offered me a contract. She knew why they wanted to change my name."

Hazel's advice?

"Don't do it."

Creighton concurs.

"I am *not* Lon Chaney, Junior," he adamantly states to writer Helen Louise Walker. "If my father had wanted me to have that name, he would have given it to me."

Studio executives try to change his mind, pointing out that he's never appeared on stage or screen.

He insists he'd rather go back to his old job than change his moniker.

"If I go into the movies, I'll use my own name, not that of my father," Chaney tells the Associated Press on January 27.

Then, MGM weighs in. They're very much against Creighton changing his name since his father's movies are still being run in the provinces.

Other Hollywood power players are against the idea as well.

"Creighton Chaney has a long way to go before he can emulate his distinguished father," gossip columnist Louella Parsons writes.

Small reopens negotiations. RKO makes a new offer: they'll sign him as Creighton Chaney for five years—with yearly options—at $200 a week. The potential still exists for him to make $3500 a week down the line. This is the contract he inks on his birthday.

"No actor could ever become a real successor to dad—much less a punk like me," Chaney explains to NEA Service Writer Dan Thomas. "I don't know if I ever will make the grade in pictures. Executives at RKO who signed me to a contract apparently think I can. But that still is to be proven…I am not going to be a character actor—at least not for some years yet. That is the most difficult type of acting, and I want some years of experience before even attempting it. Right now, I want just straight roles so I can learn what acting is all about."

Most of the press responds favorably to Chaney's idealistic insistence on keeping his own name.

"Virtue still has the habit of self-reward," applauds Lee Shippey in *The Los Angeles Times* on February 7, "and the publicity attending his persistent refusal probably equals in volume and certainly surpasses in value that which he would have received by consenting to adopt his father's name."

But a few commentators are more cynical.

"Creighton Chaney is to be admired for insisting that his screen debut be under his own name rather than Lon Chaney, Jr.," *The Manhattan Mercury* in Kansas opines on February 16, "but exhibitors doubtless will take his resolution merely as a nice gesture. The studio will list 'Creighton Chaney' in its casts when he is used, but theaters will put 'Lon Chaney, Jr.' on their marquees—or else this movie business has taken on a delicate nicety we've not suspected."

Meanwhile, Louella Parsons predicts Chaney won't have much of a career at all.

"The odds are against him," she writes on May 1. "This is a rather bitter thing to say at the very beginning of a career, but I say the odds are against him because it's the most difficult thing in the world for a child of a famous star to carve a name for himself or herself in the same line of work.

"Outsiders who cannot get into the studios will look at Young Chaney with envy," she correctly points out, "with the feeling that he is trading on his father's name. He will have to be just a little better than if he hadn't had Lon Chaney for a father. It's true he might never have had his opportunity at radio studio [sic] if he had not been born the son of Lon Chaney, but once in the studio the going is not easy."

Nobody knows this better than Creighton.

"I don't know whether I'm an actor," he candidly admits to columnist Hubbard Keavy. "An 18-page contract calls me an 'artist,' but that doesn't make me one."

Before long, he'll be subjected to endless questions about—and comparisons to—his father. He'll deal with this at first, but it will get old fast.

Meanwhile, in March, RKO has him start acting lessons with Albert Lovejoy, formerly a drama coach at Harvard.

Soon, it's announced that his first film role will be a bit part in *Bird of Paradise*, to be directed by King Vidor on location in Hawaii.

Creighton Chaney will be making motion pictures whether Pop would have approved or not.

* * *

Hazel Chaney is not feeling well. She's tired all the time and is scared of dying. She can no longer handle the day-to-day tasks that come with being in charge of Lon's estate. Something has to give.

Though it breaks her heart, she begins downsizing by selling the stone ranch house in Big Pine. John Jeske handles the details.

The news of the sale boils Creighton's blood. Once again, he's denied—unjustly, in his opinion—an important piece of his father's wealth. And once again, Jeske has been instrumental in robbing him.

Creighton is already a drinker. But he hits the bottle harder now.

Meanwhile, RKO gets the publicity machine moving for him. Tall, powerfully built, and tan—with beautifully expressive eyes—these are the peak years for Chaney's looks. The studio decides to market him as a heartthrob.

They also plant various tidbits about him in news-papers.

For example, following his bit role in *Bird of Paradise* (among others), he gets his first starring role in the serial *The Last Frontier*.

"The young man is 6 feet 2 in height and considerably good-looking," Irene Thirer gushes on June 20.

It's also announced that he will be playing a substantial part in *The Most Dangerous Game*.[2]

"It looks as though Creighton Chaney, son of the late Lon Chaney, is going to win his spurs all on his own efforts and talent," notes *The Los Angeles Times*.

Along the way, he manages to teach fellow actor—and *Bird of Paradise* star—Joel McCrea how to wrestle. McCrae needs the skills for an upcoming role in *Sport Page*.[3]

Not all the news is human interest fluff. On May 4, *The Los Angeles Times* reports that Chaney's son Lon Ralph has been injured. It seems that while the gardener was mowing the lawn, the 4-year-old decided it would be a good idea to stick his hands in the blades, necessitating a trip to Hollywood Receiving Hospital and four stitches.

By summer, Chaney is starring as The Black Ghost, the masked hero in *The Last Frontier*. The shoot is no picnic.

"I'd never really ridden a horse—not to barge out and jump on one and ride like the devil," he'll recall in later years. "And the first thing they had me do was to get twenty feet[4] up in a tree and leap on the villain as he galloped beneath me."

He breaks a thumb and a rib, and dislocates his hip in the process. Later, he throws his shoulder out performing a stunt in the rapids. He claims he didn't bother to see a doctor.

Why not use a stunt man?

"My dad would feel disgraced at the idea of a double for a Chaney," he explains.

Upon its release in September, both the serial and Chaney garner decent revues.

"The heroic building of a new empire is told in a hurricane of magnificent spectacle and hair-raising feats, starring Creighton Chaney, son of the late Lon Chaney," notes the *News-Journal*.

In November, we're told that "Creighton Chaney's the most kissed man in Hollywood," thanks to the fact that RKO uses him in screen tests opposite potential starlets.[5]

But he's not just kissing in front of the camera.

When he isn't drunk, Chaney can be very attentive and charming. He has a real sense of humor and a way of telling funny stories. There's a good-hearted side to him that's as fully ingrained in him as are his insecurities. Women find him to be attractive.

With strife at home, and no end to the pretty faces at the studio, Chaney—like Cleva before him—indulges in a series of extramarital affairs.

And then, October brings horrible news.

Hazel is dying of breast cancer.

October 31, 1933

Halloween. Hazel Bennett Hastings Chaney is dead at 46.[1]

This is the climax of what can only be described as a terrible year in Creighton Chaney's life.

The troubles begin in January when RKO drops him.

"Gwili Andre, Creighton Chaney and Julie Haydon, three young players who joined Radio with much ballyhoo, are not having their contracts renewed," Louella Parsons announces to the world on January 27. "Creighton Chaney did not measure up to expectations...That does not mean that these three will not register in motion pictures at other studios. It merely means they are through at Radio."

As noted previously, RKO has attempted to market Chaney as a leading man in the manner of Clark Gable, to whom he's sometimes compared...in print, anyway.

Chaney prefers this to being sized up next to his Pop.

"Don't say anything comparing me with my father," he pleads with Nancy Pryor of *Movie Classic* magazine. "There isn't any comparison between us. Dad was an artist—a real actor. I'm just a fellow trying to get along in the movies. I'd rather be compared to anybody else but my dad, because I know I'm not worthy of that comparison."

He goes on to say that he welcomes being told that he's similar to Gable…but not because he's vain.

"I figured that if I was being compared to Mr. Gable, it would sidetrack other comparisons to my dad," he explains.

To look more like a leading man, Chaney decides to lose some weight. He drops from 215 pounds to 180 by going on a diet of fruit juice and running five miles a day.

"Young Chaney lost not one ounce of fat in that reduction!" gushes Pryor. "There wasn't any fat on him. His entire two hundred and fifteen pounds were solid muscle."

He'll never be as thin again.[2]

But even as Pryor is writing this puff piece, RKO is deciding that Chaney isn't a good fit for them. Because of his performance in *The Last Frontier*, studio suits believe his real potential is in cheap westerns. It's revealing that Pryor notes, "He is tall and dark with nice eyes, particularly nice when he smiles, which he doesn't often do."

You have to be happy to smile.

RKO determines to have him play out his remaining pictures in the saddle.

* * *

In February, columnist Wood Soanes finds Chaney making *Lucky Devils* with veteran actor Bill Boyd. The film is about stuntmen.

Chaney is complaining. Ironically, it seems he's going to be stunt-doubled in a scene and he's not happy.

"Don't be a sap," Boyd advises. "These boys know how to take the fall. You may be in swell condition, but if you don't know the tricks of the trade, you're heading for the hospital."

Chaney's not convinced.

"I can do most of the things a stunt man does," he says to Soanes. "Anyway, there's a tradition in our family. We take our own knocks and don't pass them on."

When director Ralph Ince prepares to film a dangerous fire-and-rescue scene, Chaney insists that he wants to do the stunts.

Ince is having none of it.

"Let the stunt man earn a living too," he says.

* * *

October 14, 1933. Los Angeles.

A dark-haired man with a thin mustache and thick glasses arrives at the marriage license bureau. He wants to file a notice of intent to marry.

What's the bride's name? Hazel Chaney.

Since Hazel isn't with him, Rosamond Rice—who heads the bureau—decides to question the man.

She learns that Hazel Chaney is deathly ill, and is currently being cared for at St. Vincent's Hospital.[3]

"I told the man that if he would get a doctor's certificate of her illness, a notice could be filed and a license issued in three days," Rice tells reporters.

The dark-haired man is, of course, John Jeske.

And he doesn't know if Hazel will even survive for the next three days. C.G. Toland, her doctor, doesn't believe that recovery is in the cards.

With no other choice, Jeske takes a blank form and leaves.

The story gets out quickly—LON CHANEY'S WIDOW TO MARRY!

The Los Angeles Times contacts Creighton for comment. He's understandably shocked and upset by the news.

"I know absolutely nothing about this marriage plan," he thunders, "and you'll have to ask Mr. Jeske about that. I have not been able to see my mother for several weeks, I am told, due to her illness."[4]

Creighton refuses to make any further comments, but it's easy to imagine what's going through his mind...

What the hell is Jeske up to now? And what's going on with the woman he still considers to be his mother?

The Times tries to reach Jeske, but no luck. They do, however, stumble across the reason for the proposed nuptials: what's left of Lon Chaney's estate.

I've heard talk about the marriage being a kind of reward for Jeske's longtime service to the Chaneys, Dr. Toland tells Rice. But there are family objections.

Translation: Hazel plans to give her sizable inheritance to Jeske rather than her stepson. And a marriage is an ironclad way of doing just that.[5]

The Times runs the story the very next day. Hazel is crushed by the publicity.

Creighton is crushed too. He feels betrayed yet again—potentially shut out of his father's estate once more, and—in his view—cut off from Hazel by Jeske.

Why does everyone hate him so much?

It doesn't help that *The Times* runs this nugget in the story:

> "Jeske was for many years **make-up man for Chaney** during his long and spectacular career of grotesque characters. Jeske also acted in the capacity of a man-of-all-jobs around the Chaney home and acted as a general confidential secretary" [*emphasis mine*].

Creighton is infuriated. Now Jeske is claiming to have been Pop's makeup man?

When the assertion is repeated in a later edition of *The Times*, Creighton rings up Read Kendall, the organization's Hollywood columnist.

Listen, he says to Kendall, my father never employed Jeske as a makeup man. He was never aided by anyone when he prepped his screen roles, except for a butler who helped him dress.

"I am making this statement at such a late date because I am sick and tired of people trying to cash in on my father's fame when it is not due them," he states.

Meanwhile, with marriage off the table—the publicity they've generated is horrible, after all—Hazel and Jeske have to make other plans. And quick.

Jeske meets with Hazel's attorneys. They hammer out what they hope will be an airtight will. Hazel signs on October 17, just two weeks before she dies.

John Jeske is at her bedside when she passes.

When her will is read on November 8, Jeske receives $10,000, plus stocks, bonds, and real estate. He also scores furniture and tableware.

Among other things, Hazel leaves her sister a house and St. Ambrose Catholic Church $500.

In contrast—though she mentions, "that by a former marriage my late husband left surviving him one child, to wit, Creighton Chaney"—she bequeaths nothing to her stepson.

In closing, she stipulates that anyone who decides to challenge her will is to be awarded $1.

Is Hazel here treating Creighton in the same way that her husband treated Cleva? It sure seems that way to him.

In a boiling rage—fueled by years of feeling of inadequate and betrayed—Creighton tracks Jeske down and confronts him.

The situation is a tinderbox because, as gentle as Creighton can be, he is more than capable of physical violence, particularly when drinking. And Jeske is no match for him.

The air turns blue. No holds are barred. Creighton out-and-out accuses Jeske of trying to marry Hazel to grab his father's dough.

Amazingly, Jeske is able to talk him down just enough to survive.

But Chaney is not through. Next, he attacks Hazel's attorneys, haranguing them for hours and threatening a lawsuit.

By December, cooler heads prevail. Jeske and Hazel's legal team decide to deal Creighton in. He's to receive his father's furniture, car, and fishing rods, plus $2500 in cash.

Jeske, however, retains some prize real estate, including five lots in Placerville.

Chaney intends to get those too, no matter how long it takes.

After all, *he's* family. Jeske is just some interloping "foreigner."

Right?

June 25, 1936

Superior Court, Los Angeles.

Dorothy H. Chaney is suing Creighton T. Chaney for divorce. The grounds? Extreme cruelty.

Dorothy tells the court that her husband drinks heavily. A lot of times, he doesn't come home until the wee hours. Sometimes, he doesn't come home at all. And when he is home, he's sullen and sarcastic.

Ralph L. Hinckley, Dorothy's father, backs up her testimony.

Neither mention Chaney's numerous affairs.

Creighton's only comment is, "Sorry it had to happen."

A property settlement has been hammered out previous to trial. Dorothy is granted an uncontested decree of divorce. She gets custody of Lon Ralph, now 7, and Ron, age 6. Chaney turns over all community property to her. In addition, he must pay her 20% of all the money he makes over $3600 per year, to a maximum of $1200.

Apparently, Chaney has decided to throw everything at her—including the kitchen sink—just to get out of the marriage. Is he that unhappy? Or that guilty? Is he paying her off to keep her quiet about his adultery?

Whatever the reason—like Cleva before him—Creighton walks away from the marriage with nothing.

And there are harder times coming.

* * *

His divorce is not an isolated incident. Chaney has been on a collision course with disaster since being dropped by RKO in early 1933.

He gets bit parts in cheap, independently produced westerns. When he holds out for something better, there are no offers.

"I'll swear I spoke the line, 'So you won't talk, eh?' at least fifty times," he'll gripe later, "and I'd rather not think about how often I had to say, 'Don't shoot him now—I have a better plan!'"

By 1934, things on the home front are no better. Dorothy knows that her husband is unfaithful. She probably takes small comfort in the fact that the affairs are emotionally meaningless, though she is obviously still hurt. But there are two sons in the picture—sons that Creighton dotes on when he's home. Can there be any doubt that she feels trapped in a Devil's Bargain for the sake of the children?

Meanwhile, though he's far from being a Hollywood star, there are still some tidbits about Creighton that make the newspapers.

One such item in the *Santa Rosa Republican* notes that Chaney's litter of ten Doberman puppies are worth $1500, just shy of $30,000 today.

Another item notes that he's had to testify in a damage suit regarding contract rights to a film he's making called *Within the Rock*.

But the most shocking Chaney-related story of 1934 occurs in July when John Jeske is kidnapped.

* * *

For Jeske, life has been good since Hazel's death.

He's managed to pay off all estate debts. And he's recently gotten married to the former Elaine Beuter.

But Jeske has hardly stayed under the radar. He's spent much of his inheritance money on fancy clothes and a new car. He is not above flashing wads of cash in public.

And because he brokered the deal between Hazel and the buyer of the stone ranch house in Big Pine, he's allowed to stay there as well when the new owners aren't present.

This gets Joy Parker's attention.

Parker had been an acquaintance of Lon Chaney's, and had cared for Hazel during her illness. Being left out of Hazel's will, however, has angered her.

Much like Creighton Chaney, Parker blames Jeske.[1]

She decides to squeeze some money out of him. She recruits her husband Lynn, plus their friends Floyd Britton, Ida May Alameda, Cyril Russell, Manuel Cordoza, and George Dorsey.

A plan is set in motion.

* * *

On July 16, Jeske and his wife are relaxing at the house in Big Pine.

After dark, there is a knock at the door. A man claims to have a package for Jeske.

"Oh, fine," Jeske says.

When Jeske opens the door, he's staring at two men, each holding a gun in both hands.

The men bind and gag Jeske, then bring Elaine into the living room and gag her, too. They want the money and ring Hazel Chaney left to Jeske. At this point, however, Jeske has not received any money, and he's already sold the ring.

One of the gunmen shoves his pistol into Jeske's mouth.

After two hours, Jeske manages to convince his captors that he's telling the truth. Searching the room, one of the kidnappers discovers Jeske's checkbook. It shows a balance of $91.

Write a check out for $76 cash, a gunman instructs.

They ransack the cabin, stealing some rifles, a suitcase, and Elaine's jacket. They then pile the Jeskes in a car with another woman and drive them to Los Angeles. By the time they get to Parker's house, they've been joined by the rest of the crew. The Jeskes spend the night hostage in Parker's garage.

The next day, the captors bring Jeske to a Hollywood bank. He cashes the $76 check and turns the cash over to them. Amazingly, the kidnappers release the couple in Hollywood Hills. The Jeskes make their way to their apartment.

Once they get home, the phone rings.

It's the kidnappers. They want $50 to return Jeske's watch and his wife's ring.

The cops are called. They plant officers in Jeske's apartment. Then they wait.

The phone rings. The kidnappers instruct Jeske to meet them at Tenth and Hill Streets for the handoff.

The cops are there to arrest them when they arrive.

On September 14, Alameda, Britton, and Russell are sentenced to life without parole. Dorsey and Cordoza are handed seven-years-to-life in Folsom.

On October 5, the Parkers—claiming to be innocent—are sentenced to life as well. The judge squashes any possibility of parole.

"Let this be a ringing message that such vicious criminals can expect no mercy from the courts," he says.

Jeske's wife will leave him less than a year later.

While Creighton must take some pleasure in the fact that Jeske has been put through the ringer, the publicity surrounding the kidnapping aggravates him. As long as Jeske lives, Creighton will have a constant reminder that both his father and stepmother chose a stranger—"a foreigner!"—as their confidant rather than their son.

The very thought of this eats him alive.

* * *

Professionally, Chaney continues to struggle. Tired of being offered bits in an unsteady stream of pathetic horse operas, he decides to try the stage. He takes lessons in Oliver Hinsdell's drama school over at MGM, becoming what the *Napa Journal* calls "a new type, part heavy, part comedy."

When he's showcased at Laboratory playlets in Beverly Hills, he attracts the attention of some studio executives.

But the major break is yet to come.

Late in the year, Creighton's seemingly impossible situation has him thinking the unthinkable: should he change his name to Lon Chaney, Jr.?

For Creighton, this is a horrible question to wrestle with. He's publicly ridiculed the very idea for the last two years. He fiercely wants to cut out his own identity, whatever that may be. And while in public he's always praised his father, events since Pop's death have rocked Creighton's image of him.

Plus, how can he top his father if he has to take Dad's name? Will this lock him up in his father's shadow? Isn't this admitting defeat—something the Chaneys are loathe to do? How will he look at himself in the mirror?

As of January 2, 1935, he's still towing the party line.

"I'm honestly grateful to them [*the studios*] for giving me a chance to make good under my own steam as Creighton Chaney," he tells *The Hollywood Report*. "I figure they must feel that I have something to offer of my own."

But by January 4, he's changed his mind.

It's a Devil's Bargain of his own. As such, he tries to put the best possible spin on it.

"During the two years I've been in pictures, producers and directors have continued to tell me I have ability, but lack the box-office attraction of a *name*," he tells the Associated Press. "In those two years I have played in eight pictures, and have done, I think, fairly well."

He goes on to say that he believes the name change will offer him more opportunity.

Behind the scenes, of course, he hates what he's done. What does this say about him? How could he have caved? Is this the weakness in him that Pop feared?

"They starved me into it," he'll often complain, attempting to save face. "After that, I had a chance at least."

Sadly, he's wrong.

He scores one lead in 1935 in a film called *Scream in the Night*, which isn't released until 1943. He gets four bits in 1936.

He's changed his name for this?

* * *

January 1936. Chaney is approached by his friend Gertrude M. Davey.[2]

Tall, thin, and very attractive, the dark-haired Davey is a former Mack Sennett Bathing Beauty. But her show biz career is over, and she's now running a café on Melrose Avenue in Los Angeles.

The trouble is, she's going broke.

Her proposal to Chaney? Let's rename the place THE LON CHANEY JR. CAFÉ and get a liquor license.

Perhaps reasoning that he has to get at least *some* use out of the name, Chaney advances Davey the money, signs the application for a liquor license, and becomes a partner in the venture.[3]

The café does reasonably well for a while. Davey is the on-site point person, though she'll indicate in court later that Chaney is involved as well.

And then in April, the café's liquor license is pulled. It seems the establishment is serving booze too close to Fairfax High School.

On May 1, Chaney hears the license won't be renewed. Seeing the handwriting on the wall, he gives notice to Davey and all creditors that he's bailing out.

Davey decides to try to renew the license on her own.

* * *

March 8, 1936. *The Kingsport Times* publishes a small blurb on Chaney in connection to a showing of *Within the Rock*:

"Players who performed with his father are a unit in declaring that Creighton is a 'perfect chip of the old block,' who displays unconsciously many of the mannerisms, and much of the stage presence which lent such peculiar grace to Lon Chaney's performances. But the son has undoubtedly 'made good on his own'…it required considerable art and address on Creighton Chaney's part to create the necessary sympathy for the character he was impersonating. That he succeeded in so doing speaks volumes for the cleverness of the young actor."

If Chaney ever reads the piece, he must be pleased by the praise…but aggravated that he's not referred to by his current professional name.[4]

It's also at this time that Chaney reconnects with Patricia Beck. As it happens, Chaney's waiting out a rain storm on set when his friend Oliver Drake comes by.

Let's go see a couple of girls I know, Drake suggests to Chaney.

Lo and behold, one of them is Patsy.

The petite, red-haired, 24-year-old is a commercial model and sometime film extra. However, she's been souring on the business since 1935. The final straw occurs when she agrees to appear at the Hollywood Minsky Music Hall…then finds out what's expected from her on stage. Horrified, she promptly quits, demanding that management take down her promotional photo.

When they don't, she sues them for $1975, claiming "great humiliation, mortification and embarrassment, [that] has damaged her reputation."

She and Chaney hit it off. Lon tells Drake that he plans to divorce Dorothy and marry Patsy.[5]

* * *

June 18, 1936. *The Los Angeles Times* reports that Gertrude Davey is testifying in a hearing regarding attempted bribery over a liquor license for the Lon Chaney, Jr. Café.

In seeking the renewal, Davey swears, she's been put in touch with two local "fixers": Erwin P. "Pete" Werner, an attorney, and his wife Helen—known as "Queen Helen" thanks to her influential political connections.

According to Davey, the Werners have asked for $1000 to prime the right pumps in Sacramento.

Davey—believing the café is "marked for a shakedown" because of the name "Lon Chaney, Jr."—objects to the price. She believes the Werners are trying to take advantage of her because they think Chaney is wealthy. She claims they'd settled on $500—$250 up front, $250 upon delivery.

The Werners deny her story. Queen Helen says she's never met Davey at all. Pete says Davey gave him $250 as a retainer for his services as an attorney.

"I wanted a license," Davey responds. "I didn't want an attorney."

Needless to say, the license never materializes.

Chaney is made aware of the sordid affair, and on June 6, issues a statement via his own lawyer. He admits to knowing Davey, to bankrolling the café, and to signing for the liquor license. But he claims to have gotten out of the venture, "On or about May 1, this year."

> "I personally made no attempt to procure a renewal of the liquor license…Since that time I have had no business relations with Gertrude M. Davey and was not party in any sense whatsoever to the procuring of a renewal of the liquor license by her. I was not instrumental in the obtaining of the renewal of the liquor license nor did I advance any money for the renewal of the same to Gertrude M. Davey or any other person who may have contacted her in obtaining the new license."

By June, of course, it's a matter for the court…and the newspapers. Chaney's name is dragged into every article. Once again, this is publicity he doesn't want.

Things get more tense when Davey claims to have been accosted on the street by two men after testifying. She's assigned a police guard as a result.

The case drags on until March 5, 1937 when the jury acquits both Queen Helen and Pete Werner.

* * *

Chaney's divorce from Dorothy leaves them both bitter.

"I think it was a very painful divorce," Ronald Curt Chaney—Chaney's grandson—will explain to *Biography* in 1995. "I think she was very hurt by it. They never talked about each other too much, I think because of the pain of the divorce, and the split-up of the family also."

The breakup has left him financially destitute. At one point, he claims to have starved for four days.

"People who might have helped me didn't," he'll say years later.

His career is sputtering, too.

"Creighton Chaney, son of the late Lon, started out with the admirable intention of remaining Creighton Chaney, but later became 'Lon Chaney, Jr.'," notes the *Abilene Reporter-News* on February 23, 1937. "As such, he has been fairly constantly employed, but the unique stardom of his father is not his."

Increasingly, he leans on Patsy Beck.

Then, in the summer of 1937, comes a much-needed break: he signs a contract with 20th Century Fox. They promise him meaningful character roles.

Are things finally looking up?

Chaney crosses his thick fingers.

* * *

Friday, October 1, 1937. Colton, California in San Bernardino county.

Chaney and Patsy elope. The Reverend W. H. Richmond of the First Presbyterian Church officiates.

Despite his recent Fox contract, Chaney is so broke at this point that Patsy's wedding band is silver. It comes at a cost of $6.

Along for the ride to witness the ceremony are actors Astrid Allwyn and Robert Kent. The newly-married Chaneys swear them to secrecy—"to put one over on the gossips"[6]—then embark on a trailer honeymoon. They make their home in Van Nuys.

By January 10, they have a change of heart and contact the media to announce their marriage.

"It's possible to keep a secret in Hollywood after all," Chaney laughs.

United Press blurbs oddly refer to Patsy as "a non-professional." And the endless comparisons to Chaney's father surface yet again.

"Chaney has acted in films, but with none of the fame of his late father," the *Appeal-Democrat* notes, somewhat cruelly.

The marriage will endure until Chaney's death, nearly 36 years later. But it will be a rocky one. Chaney's penchant for violence while drinking will only increase,[7] and there will be whispers in the future that he abuses his wife.[8]

For better or worse, Patsy will concentrate on Chaney's good qualities—his humor, his sweetness, his love of children and animals—to make the marriage last.

She will learn to comfort him when she can, and enable him when she can't.⁹ This will include tolerating his constant drinking and occasional affairs.¹⁰

* * *

As 1938 dawns, Fox is happy enough with Chaney to pick up his option.

But the studio's promise of meaningful character roles has yet to bear fruit. Sure, he's appeared in no less than seventeen films in 1937, but eleven of those are bits without screen credit. And he's certainly not the star in any of the other six.

The situation repeats itself in 1938. Chaney will make twelve films, and receive credit for five of them.

Which is worse? Starving? Or a meaningless grind like this?

Before long, the choice will be made for him.

* * *

Saturday, July 30, 1938. An interesting item appears in George Adams' syndicated "Today's Talk" column:

> "[I]t seems that Lon Chaney, Jr., playing a marine sergeant in Twentieth Century's *Wooden Anchors*, was sent to United Costumers to be fitted with a uniform. After trying several, he finally found one that

fitted perfectly save for the sleeves, which needed lengthening. Stripping off the coat, he happened to glance inside—and blinked. On the lining were these words, printed in ink: 'This coat worn by me, Lon Chaney, in *Tell It to the Marines.*'"

The reports on October 13 aren't as beguiling. Chaney has almost been killed on location. *The Winnipeg Tribune* trumpets:

> "Lon Chaney, Jr., noted young actor, missed death by a hair's breadth during the filming of a spectacular train robbery sequence for the 20th Century Fox Technicolor production, *Jesse James.*"

The film—starring Tyrone Power and Henry Fonda—is being made on location in Pineville, Missouri by director Henry King at a cost of $1.6 million—a bit less than $30 million today.

Chaney, by now weighing more than 200 pounds again, has grown a thick beard for his role. He'll take thirty-first billing as "One of James Gang."

He's mounted on a horse and racing the train at breakneck speed when the cinch on his saddle breaks.

Chaney slams into the train, then crashes to the ground. His startled horse rears back and plants a hoof directly on Chaney's leg. In agony but still conscious, Chaney quickly rolls away from the track before the train can run him over.

He's rushed to a hospital in Joplin where X-rays are taken. Luckily, his leg isn't broken, but his ligaments have been torn.

King—already in a foul mood thanks to a nagging earache—angrily blames Chaney's drinking for the accident and sends him home.

January 27, 1939. *Jesse James* is released. It's a sizable hit, and will go on to become the third highest-grossing film of the year.[11]

But it does Lon Chaney Jr. no good. By the time the film comes out, he's been dropped by 20th Century Fox.

* * *

Tuesday, December 20, 1938. Superior Court.

Chaney and his former wife Dorothy face off again.

The origin of this current turmoil relates back to their settlement in 1936. Dorothy had been granted the interest in a $36,000 note held by her father. Since then, however, the interest rate has depreciated from nine to seven percent. This is a loss Dorothy claims she can't afford.

Dorothy files charges. She says Chaney needs to ante up to support her and their sons.

Chaney—still wearing the beard he explains he's grown for *Jesse James*—pleads poverty himself. He testifies that giving her the house, furniture, and interest in the note made him believe that she was "amply provided for."

Since that time, he says, I've given little thought to her financial condition.

As to his own finances, he claims to have less than $100 in savings. He also says he's earned only about $3600[12] in 1938, and that his prospects for 1939 aren't good.

But his appeals fall on deaf ears. Judge Leslie E. Still orders him to pay $50 a month.

It can't help that the related International News Service reports describe him as "a film extra."

Soon after this court appearance, his car and furniture are repossessed.

Where, exactly, is rock bottom?

October 27, 1941

"So you're the gal who swiped my dressing room," Lon Chaney, Jr. says, annoyed. "You took it away from Brod Crawford and me—I think that was a hell of a thing to do!"

It's the first day of shooting on *The Wolf Man* at Universal Studios. The object of Chaney's wrath is his co-star, Evelyn Ankers.

Ankers has recently turned 23. Born in Chile to English parents, she begins acting in British films in the 1930s. By 1940, she's performing on Broadway in New York. Twentieth Century Fox, Warner Brothers, and Universal all take an interest in the pretty, blonde, blue-eyed actress.

She signs a contract with Fox at first. But when they don't pick up her option, she heads over to Universal.

The Wolf Man is Ankers' fifth film at her new home. She's just finished working with Chaney and Crawford on *North to the Klondike*, during which time they've earned her disapproval—Crawford by bruising her arm with a 'hello punch,' and Chaney by laughing at her tears. A few days before cameras turn on *The Wolf Man*, the suits let her know that they're giving her a beautiful new dressing room—a reward for her great work, they say. She has no idea it's been taken from Chaney and Crawford, both of whom are bullies, at least in her estimation.

By this time, Ankers has survived the terror of working with The Dead End Kids and Abbott and Costello. So when Chaney declares that swiping the dressing room was a hell of a thing to do, she knows exactly how to handle the situation.

She agrees with him.

"He seemed to have a need to be liked by people," she'll accurately note years later.

An uneasy peace is established between them.

For now.

* * *

Chaney's road from repossession to a lucrative contract—and possible stardom—has been filled with potholes. In the depths of despair as 1939 dawned, Chaney could never have imagined being where he is now in 1941...even if he *is* upset about his dressing room.

The journey begins inauspiciously early in 1939. There are plans in the works to remake *The Hunchback of Notre Dame* over at RKO. When Chaney hears, he gets excited. Quasimodo could be his dream role. True, he wasn't thrilled with his first RKO experience, but this remake gives him an opportunity to go head-to-head with Pop at last...and possibly top him.

Because the film is a talkie, the younger Chaney believes he'll have the advantage.

"We're two different personalities," he'll explain in 1952. "Dad, for instance, couldn't read a speech of over a paragraph if he had to. It wasn't necessary in those days. On the other hand, he could do things with his eyes and even with flexing his facial muscles that I would never be able to duplicate. Also, he was a little guy, while I'm as big as this year's income tax."[1]

Chaney tests for the part. Reportedly, RKO is pleased. But there are others in the mix, particularly the Englishman Charles Laughton.[2] Laughton, however, is having U.S. tax issues which might prevent him from taking the role. If Laughton can't do it, RKO pledges to go with Chaney.

For better or worse, Laughton clears up the problem. He gives a marvelous performance in the resultant film.

Chaney goes back to deprivation.

He'll later claim that he and Patsy have gone hungry for 24 hours when his agent shows up with an offer: an audition for the west coast stage version of John Steinbeck's *Of Mice and Men*.[3]

The play is based on the best-selling novel. Steinbeck himself has done the adaptation for the stage. It's a tragic tale of two bindle stiffs—the small, quick-witted George Milton, and the huge, simple-minded Lennie Small—who desire a little piece of the American Dream for themselves. Sadly, Lennie's great strength, coupled with his disability, keep the pair in perpetual hot water.

When *Of Mice and Men* opens at the Music Box Theatre on Broadway in November 1937, it's a hit, running for more than 200 performances. In these pre-Tony days, *Mice* is named Best Play by the New York Drama Critics' Circle.

Five of the New York players are set to reprise their parts at the 1100-seat El Capitan Theater on Hollywood Boulevard.[4]

But Brod Crawford as Lennie is not among them.

William Broderick Crawford, 28, is five-eleven and built as solidly as a fire hydrant. Like Chaney, he's the product of a Show Biz family—his father was in Vaudeville, and his mom acted on stage. Like Chaney, he's a hard-drinking chain smoker who's as strong as an ox.

Unlike Chaney, he'll eventually score an Oscar for Best Actor as Willie Stark in *All the King's Men* (1949).

Eventually, he and Chaney will become fast friends. But for now, Crawford ditches the play in favor of film roles at Goldwyn and Columbia. Thus, opportunity knocks, and Chaney can test for Lennie.

Chaney balks at first. Though he's a reader—he loves Zane Grey, for example—he's never read *Of Mice and Men*. He has only the slightest idea of what Lennie's supposed to be all about.

But he pushes himself and reports to the El Capitan. By his own admission, the audition goes poorly. But Wallace Ford (*Freaks*)—producing the play and acting the part of George—sees something in Chaney: great physical strength coupled with tragedy lurking in his sad eyes, perhaps?

He rolls the dice. Chaney gets the part.

Chaney hasn't done any stage acting since 1934. And that was in *playlets*. Now, he's got a huge part with a number of lines. How should Lennie sound? How should he walk? How is Chaney ever going to get through this?

Patsy runs the dialogue with him over and over as he fleshes out the part.

Opening night has him shaking in his boots. But when it's done—when Lennie has been mercy-killed by his best friend and mentor in order to save him from a lynch mob—the applause can't be any louder.

There are fourteen curtain calls. *Fourteen!*

There are very few completely happy days in Chaney's life.

But this is one of them.

* * *

With the play a bona fide hit, Steinbeck's stock rises in Hollywood.

John Ford, for example, is prepping a film version of Steinbeck's controversial bestseller *The Grapes of Wrath* over at 20th Century Fox. He plans to begin in October. Hank Fonda is slated to star.

Meanwhile, Lewis Milestone—Oscar-winning director of Universal's 1930 Best Picture winner *All Quiet on the Western Front*—is getting ready to put *Of Mice and Men* in front of the cameras at United Artists in

August. The producer is Hal Roach, who has secured the $250,000 budget.

Though Roach wants James Cagney or Humphrey Bogart for George, Burgess "Buzzy" Meredith, 31—and no stranger on Broadway—is hired instead. Bette Field, 26, and also a Broadway veteran, will eventually win the part of the tragic Mae.[5]

And Milestone has 40-year-old Guinn "Big Boy" Williams—so nicknamed for his muscular build and 6'2" height—set to forsake his usual Westerns in the role of Lennie.

"I had made up my mind who should play all the featured roles, Lennie included," Milestone explains. "Everyone in town knew that."

Everyone, that is, except Chaney, who shows up unexpectedly in Milestone's office one day.

"Can't I have a test?"

Caught off guard, the 43-year-old director agrees.

But first, there are previously scheduled screen tests to get through. Cashing in on Chaney's enthusiasm, Milestone has him read Lennie's lines opposite other hopeful actors and actresses.

"When the time came to test him, I didn't have to," Milestone remarks. "I couldn't see anybody else in the part."[6]

In preparation for shooting, Patsy's beautician dyes Chaney's hair red, and he's costumed in denim. He also wears elevator shoes that increase his height by six inches.

The Agoura Ranch set is built on a lot—rented from newspaper titan William Randolph Hearst—in a little more than a week, and shooting begins.

According to Patsy Chaney—who visits the set frequently—Milestone feels so confident in her husband's performance that he provides the actor with little or no direction.

"Go ahead and do what you want," is Milestone's frequent admonition.

Patsy believes this is because Chaney is fresh from the role on stage.

"We rehearsed a lot for it," she'll say years later.[7]

Chaney, for his part, certainly appreciates how Milestone handles him.

"They let me play Lennie my own way," he enthuses. "[He's] the biggest, sweetest, most lovable man that ever happened."

In between shots, Chaney and Buzzy Meredith bond over games of horseshoes. Their real-life rapport transfers beautifully to the film.

Magic occurs the day the company films the climatic mercy killing scene. When the smoke from the prop pistol clears and Milestone pronounces "Cut," the technicians burst into unexpected applause.

"[A] rare event for such hardened veterans who had worked with hundreds of actors," film historian Calvin Thomas Beck points out in 1975.[8]

Perhaps the key to Chaney's connection to the character—and the appreciation it generates in his coworkers—is embodied by something that Steinbeck says years later about *Mice*:

"Everyone in the world has a dream he knows can't come off, but he spends his life hoping it may."

This description certainly fits the actor who has just brought Lennie powerfully to life.

* * *

Christmas Eve, 1939. Of Mice and Men—shot in 39 days, ahead of schedule and under budget—premieres in New York. It goes into general release on February 2, 1940.

Critics are virtually unanimous in their praise.[9] They champion the film's direction, acting, story, and Aaron Copeland's musical score—his first for a motion picture.

Steinbeck is also pleased.

"[W]ent to see *Mice*," he writes his friend Elizabeth Otis, "and it is a beautiful job. Here Milestone has done a curious lyrical thing. It hangs together and is underplayed. You will like it."

Chaney himself receives raves.

"Lon Chaney, Jr. is a name to which the mass audience should respond," *Esquire* notes, "out of simple curiosity, if for no other reason. The other reason is that Chaney, Jr. is a mighty fine actor."

Variety agrees.

"Lon Chaney, Jr. dominates throughout with a fine portrayal of the childish giant," they announce in January 1940.

He's even given back-handed praise in *The Nation's* unfavorable review of the film.

'[T]hat one is never really captivated by the Lennie of Lon Chaney, Jr. is not the actor's fault," critic Franz Hoellering writes, "and it would be a gross injustice to call him the weakest of the lot. He is as good if not better than Burgess Meredith as George, but no enduring interest can be held by the repetitious, unchangeable stupidity of the character he has to play."

A still photographer on *Mice*—who had worked with Chaney's Pop—sums it up: "Like father, like son, whether he likes it or not!"

These praises provide much needed balm for an ego that has been constantly battered for almost 34 years. For a brief but glorious time, Chaney feels vindicated. Can the dream actually be coming true?

"Maybe I can get the name of Chaney back up in the theater lights across America again," he says.

It certainly looks like there are opportunities coming.

"So delighted is Hal Roach with Lon Chaney Jr.'s performance in *Of Mice and Men*...that he is closing a deal to star him in John Steinbeck's first novel, *Cup of Gold*," Louella Parsons announces on December 19, 1939. She continues:

> "[E]veryone is so glad for young Chaney who has waited a long time for the right break. There are no social problems involved in *Cup of Gold* which Steinbeck wrote about six years ago. In fact, it is a

highly adventurous pirate story—and it was Steinbeck's own idea that the yarn would be perfect for young Chaney. Like Hal, the author is delighted with Lon's work as Lennie in *Of Mice and Men*."

All concerned are feeling great about *Mice*'s prospects. *New Republic* announces, "[Y]ou can put *Of Mice and Men* down on the list of the ten best of 1940" as early as February. It will eventually be nominated for a Best Picture Oscar. Today, it is considered to be a classic film.

But in 1940, financial returns for *Of Mice and Men* are unexpectedly disappointing.

Can it be that Fox's *The Grapes of Wrath*—released at almost the same time—has oversaturated the Steinbeck market?

Whatever the case may be, plans for *Cup of Gold* are shelved.[10]

Instead, Chaney is about to do his first role under heavy makeup.

* * *

Being the son of "The Man of a Thousand Faces," it's only natural that—once Creighton Chaney gets into acting—he's asked how he feels about playing parts similar to his father's.

Back in 1932, he was dead set against the idea.

"I don't want to play the sort of roles my father did, although he was a fine actor outside of makeup," he'd told *The Los Angeles Times*. "My dad wouldn't let me come to the theater when I was a child to see him play one of those monsters, as he didn't want me to be frightened. But I ran away one day and went to see him. I didn't sleep for a week. That finished my wanting to copy him."

But back in 1932, he'd also been dead set against the idea of changing his name.

It's nearly 1940 now. He's hungry enough to have tried out for *The Hunchback of Notre Dame*. And given his success as Lennie on his own terms—a rare but great experience for him—what's the harm in a little makeup?

"I hope I never have to play another gangster or villainous cowboy the rest of my life…" Chaney tells the press. "I'd like to play heavies, if they're character parts or sympathetic. That's one of the reasons I was so happy to play Lennie on the screen. He's a heavy, but a sympathetic, understandable, human fellow and, I think, one of the grandest characters ever put on the screen…But there's one thing I hope and pray: please, no more *bad* heavies."

His upcoming role fits the bill.

With the uncredited help of D.W. Griffith,[11] Roach has put together the funds for an absurd picture called *One Million B.C.*, wherein prehistoric cave people are—anachronistically—forced to battle dinosaurs. It stars Victor Mature and Carole Landis. Roach serves as co-director with his son and Bernard Carr.

The third-billed Chaney plays Akhoba, father of Mature and King of the Rock People. Enthused by the possibilities, Chaney—like his father—decides to do his character's makeup himself.

"I would say, judging from the one or two stills that survive, he'd done a very original job on himself for *One Million B.C.*," Forrest J. Ackerman, editor of *Famous Monsters of Filmland*, will note years later. "But he wasn't allowed to use it for the film because by then the unions had come into Hollywood, and they required that a makeup man do all the makeup rather than the actor himself."

As such, Bill Madsen will turn Chaney into Akhoba. And while Madsen's work is exemplary, Ackerman gives Chaney the victory:

"Actually, I thought Chaney had done a better job on himself than the makeup man subsequently did on *One Million*, but he wasn't permitted to use that talent. It was a handicap that his father never had to face."

One Million B.C. is released on April 12, 1940 to mostly bad reviews. But it does turn a profit while launching Mature's career.

Chaney does well in the film, too. Unfortunately, Lennie has indelibly stamped him now as a different type—instead of a cowboy, casting directors see him as playing only big, strong, simple-minded guys.

"It haunts me," Chaney will complain in later years. "I get a call to play a dumb guy, and the director tells me not to be Lennie. But he's never happy until I play the part like Lennie, and then he doesn't know why he likes it!"

What Chaney doesn't realize is that his luck is about to change…again. Lennie and Akhoba have gotten the attention of executives over at Universal. A plan is being hatched.

What if they cash in on Chaney's name by putting him in a series of new horror pictures?

* * *

Late in 1940, Universal gives 46-year-old director George Waggner a screenplay called *The Electric Man*, originally written in the mid-1930s as a Boris Karloff/Bela Lugosi thriller.

See what you can do with this, Waggner is told.

Waggner—described by Evelyn Ankers as "patient, yet demanding, experimental," but always conscious that time is money—spruces up the basic tale: a decent everyman is turned into a soulless electrical killer by a mad scientist.

Waggner turns in the rewrite under his pseudonym—Joseph West—as *The Human Robot*. The suits like what he's done, and hire him to direct as well.

He's given a budget of $86,000. This is the cheapest picture Universal will make all year.

Lionel Atwill (*Mystery of the Wax Museum, Dr. X*) is brought on board to play Dr. Paul Rigas, the mad scientist. The 55-year-old actor had been a longtime heartthrob on stage, but—since the 1930s—has made his name in the movies by playing devilish villains with unique relish.[12]

The part of Dan McCormick—the human robot—is given to Lon Chaney, Jr. Universal is treating the film almost like it's a public screen test: will moviegoers accept *this* Chaney as Boris Karloff's heir?

As shooting begins, the project gets a new title: *The Mysterious Dr. R*. Universal surrounds Atwill and Chaney with Ann Nagel, Frank Albertson, and Samuel S. Hinds—all solid, believable performers.

When the character of McCormick degenerates into an electric zombie at Rigas' hands, Chaney has his first encounter with Jack P. Pierce, head of Universal's makeup department. Their relationship will eventually feature all the ups and downs of a roller coaster ride.

Born Janus Piccoula in Greece, the 51-year-old Pierce has made his reputation through the fantastic make-ups he's designed and applied on Karloff, particularly the iconic Frankenstein Monster. His methods are exact and painstaking—much like Pierce himself. He's not the friendliest of men, though he gets along very well with Dear Boris.

For *The Mysterious Dr. R*, Pierce covers Chaney's already craggy face with cotton and spirit gum, creating deep ravines that are highlighted and shadowed. When combined with John P. Fulton's pulsating glow in post-production, the effect is striking. (Interestingly, when Chaney attends a brief ceremony honoring his dad on *The Phantom of the Opera* soundstage, he's in full harness—almost like he's being anointed.)

Working quickly, Waggner completes principal photography in three weeks. The film's title is changed one final time to *Man Made Monster*. Universal execs are impressed with the results, especially since the picture has been made so fast for so little. They sign both Waggner and Chaney to seven-year deals. Chaney starts at $500 per week—worth about $9000 today—with graduated increases as his options are picked up.

Man Made Monster doesn't set the world on fire when it opens on March 18, 1941. But Chaney gets some decent notices.

"The picture has the added draw of Lon Chaney, Jr., in a monster role," *Variety* reports, "which is calculateed to whet as to the son's ability to follow in the footsteps of his father with this type of characterization. Young Chaney looks like he is on his way."

The Hollywood Reporter concurs, noting, "Chaney Jr. made a place for himself on the screen in the footsteps of his late great father."

And film historian William K. Everson will write years later that Chaney "played his fairly written role for pathos and tragedy as much as menace, and came as close as he ever would to Karloff's genius for making an audience feel sorry for him even while they feared him."

Man Made Monster even makes a small profit, and—more importantly—gives Universal confidence that Chaney can carry a film.[13]

Ambitious plans are in the works for him.

The Wolf Man is about to be born.

* * *

In 1941, Universal is not the commercial giant it will eventually become. It's not even one of the so-called Big Five movie studios in town.[14] But Chaney's salary—worth almost half-a-million bucks a year at this writing—is huge compared to what most people earn on their jobs, which allows him to enjoy creature comforts for the first time in a long time.

Not that he and Patsy are extravagant. Once they settle in their new home, they'll throw parties, but never for more than fifty guests. Most of the people who hang at the house are struggling actors and studio techs—like his Pop before him, Chaney enjoys helping these folks out. He also loves to cook—friends will rave about his broiled lamb chops with pineapple slices in Mogen David wine.[15]

Because Chaney isn't a fan of crowds, Hollywood clubbing isn't something he and Patsy do. Sure, they'll hit a restaurant or bar now and then. But when he really wants some action, he takes hunting and fishing trips up the coast…or to Florida, Canada, or Mexico. He's often accompanied by his uncle, George Chaney.

He even has a custom station wagon built which features a butane-powered refrigerator for these outings. The cost? Three thousand smackers—roughly $54,000 at this writing.

"We had a very private life," Patsy will say years later.

At Universal, Chaney is given the beautiful but infamous dressing room which he shares with none other than Brod Crawford. The two erstwhile Lennies are set to co-star in *Badlands of Dakota*, and hit it off right away.

This, of course, leads to trouble.

According to actor Robert Stack (TV's future Eliot Ness), "They were known as monsters around the Universal lot, because their drunken behavior often ended in bloodshed."

"They even had a club called The Shin-Kicking Club," actor Peter Coe recalls. "All the guys at Universal—and some of them were big and rugged like Chaney and Brod Crawford—would meet at a bar called Foster's near the studio. The whole idea was when a member greeted you with a less than big and rugged greeting, like 'Hi, Luv,' or 'Hi, Baby,' it was swiftly followed by a hard kick in the shins. If you showed any pain or let out any choice words, you had to buy a round of drinks for everybody. Believe me, when a man the size of Chaney kicks you in the shins, you end up buying a lot of drinks."

"We kidded a lot, and kicked each other with cowboy boots on," Crawford will admit with a laugh years later. "We got some exercise, but we never hit each other in the face or anything...Yeah, it was a different era completely."

Evelyn Ankers indicates that things were a little bit rougher than that.

"Every Friday or Saturday night, Lon and Brod Crawford would take bottles into their dressing room, get loaded, and then—somehow—manage to hang the furniture from the ceiling and brawl," she'll recall in later years. "On Monday, the cleaning crew was treated to a sight resembling a World War II battlefield."

When not drinking or kicking each other in the shins, they're outdoors somewhere.

"He was a good friend of mine," Crawford says. "We went on a lot of hunting and fishing trips together. We'd go deer hunting, and he was a good cook all the way around. He enjoyed that."

Crawford also gets a kick out of Chaney's sense of humor.

"He didn't tell jokes, but he told a lot of stories," Crawford notes. "Most I can't repeat."

* * *

"I want to be a great actor more than anything else in the world. I want to deserve again, many times if possible, the nomination for the Academy Award that I received for my work in *Of Mice and Men*."[16]

It's late in May, 1941, and writer Barrett C. Kiesling has found Chaney in a talking mood.

"I don't think any youngster living could have a better philosophy of life than that given me by my father," Chaney says. "It was, 'You can make any mistake in life except that of quitting too soon.'"

Will he ever make another attempt to land one of his father's signature parts?

"Certainly not. My father and I are physically and in other ways entirely different individuals. I could not do many of the things he did. But, on the other hand, with my size and my appearance, many roles are open to me that he could not have attempted. For example, he would have been miscast in *Of Mice and Men*."

* * *

Like *Man Made Monster*, the inspiration for *The Wolf Man* comes from a script that had been intended for Karloff back in 1932. By the time Universal gets around to making a werewolf film, it's 1935 and Henry Hull is the star.

But *WereWolf of London* doesn't make money, so Universal dispenses with any further attempts on the subject.

Until now.

Assigned to help bring *The Wolf Man* to life is screenwriter Curt Siodmak.

Siodmak, 39, is a native of Germany who has wisely decided that a country run by the Nazis is no place for a Jewish writer. As such, he's gotten out, and established himself in Hollywood.

"Story construction," he'll say later. "That's why I got paid in every damn country. I could construct a story out of the blue sky. Most writers are dialogue writers, and they produce very worthy dialogue, but there are really very few constructionists who started from scratch. That's why I got jobs."

Gossipy, suspicious, and a curmudgeon, Siodmak is not a really nice guy. And because he never inks a deal with Universal, he has to freelance at $400 a week. But the independence suits him, and his skills as a constructionist are undeniable.

"Though I had nothing to work with but the title *The Wolf Man*, the story fell into shape like a jigsaw puzzle," Siodmak will write years later. "I saw in it the fight of good and evil in man's soul, and the inescapable working of fate, which had also shaped my life."

Along the way, he invents many things about werewolves that people today still think come from ancient folklore: moonlight transformations, allergies to silver, and The Pentagram as "the mark of the beast," among others.

"While writing the screenplay, I became aware that all of us are subject to the whim of Harmatia, a predestined fate," he notes. "Was the Wolf Man a mirror of human life?"

Out of this rumination comes the famous lines, beginning with, "The way you walked was thorny..."

At one point, Siodmak retitles the screenplay *Destiny*, but that obviously doesn't stick. Many of his other ideas do, however.

Siodmak's tale has American technician Larry Gill coming to Talbot Castle in Wales to work on Sir John Talbot's telescope. Almost immediately, he meets and falls for Gwen Conliffe. Looking to score a date with her, he buys a silver-headed cane at her father's antique shop. While getting their fortunes told one night by a gypsy named Bela, Gwen's friend Jenny is attacked in the woods and murdered by what Gill believes to be a wolf. Killing the beast with his cane, Gill is bitten himself.

The next morning, he's told that he has—accidentally?—battered Bela to death. Scotland Yard begins to investigate.

Gill is confused at first, then becomes increasingly troubled. He knows what he killed. Or does he?

Maleva, Bela's mother, further frightens him by suggesting that—thanks to being bitten—Gill will become a werewolf himself.

The townspeople turn on him. Gwenn—who, it turns out, is engaged to a local fellow named Frank—becomes distant.

Meanwhile, Bela's funeral is a carnival celebration rather than a somber event. A tormented Gill attends, and is goaded into wrestling a trained bear. Incredibly, Gill wallops the bear and is about to kill it when Gwen steps in. Gwen and Frank proceed to argue.

Gill offers to walk her home. The two share a passionate kiss before Gwen runs off.

Then, in the middle of the night, a gravedigger is killed in the churchyard. Police find wolf tracks at the scene. When Gill wakes up in Talbot Castle the next morning, he's horrified to see wolf tracks in the garden below.

Eventually, the authorities resolve to hunt this rogue wolf. Gill decides he's leaving town. Gwen asks to go with him, but—fearing he might kill even *her*—Gill refuses.

Gill's plan is foiled when Scotland Yard stops him; his case isn't closed. He's brought back to Talbot Castle where the hunt is beginning. Gill seeks out Frank and gives him a silver bullet, instructing his rival to fire it at the beast.

Heading back through the woods, Gill begins writhing in agony. He sits on a fallen tree near a dark pool of water. The screenplay then directs:

> "And now: his forehead seems to become overgrown with fulvus grey hair—it sprouts on his cheeks—his arms become wolfishly long and thin—his teeth grow pointed and wolfish. The wolf-headed creature stares at himself, then stretches out a harry, claw-like hand, touching the surface of the clear forest pool. The water, disturbed, obfuscates the picture...The creature turns around and we only see his back. He looks like Larry from this angle, but he walks like an animal, soft-footed, wary. NOTE: The wolf-man's face is never seen—ONLY IN THE MIRROR OF THE WATER—AS SEEN THROUGH LARRY'S EYES—AS HE IMAGINES HIMSELF."

Meanwhile, Gwen has entered the woods, searching for Larry. She's overtaken by what looks like a wolf and is knocked unconscious. The beast is about to kill her when Frank fires the silver bullet.

The beast limps away, collapsing on a dead tree.

But when Frank, Sir John, and the other hunters get to the spot, they find only the lifeless Gill.

Maleva approaches. She directs Gwen to touch Gill's face with a flower, and intones a comforting chant.

"Look," Gwen says through tears as the screenplay ends. "He's smiling!"

A lot of the elements in this particular version of *The Wolf Man* are intriguing. To begin with, Chaney will be playing an American. Given the similarities between Dan McCormick and Larry Gill—plus the fact that Siodmak has written the screenplay with Chaney in mind—this is right in his wheelhouse.

Then, the idea of the wolf-man being unseen—except through Larry's eyes in a pool of water—is also interesting, in that, as many other writers have pointed out, it predates the more conceptual approach Val Lewton champions when he starts making chillers over at RKO in 1942.

But there are some logistical issues. For example, if Larry Gill *is* imagining all of this, then where, exactly, are these authentic wolf tracks coming from? And why does he look like a wolf to Frank just before Frank shoots him?

* * *

Claude Rains, the venerable 52-year-old Brit—and star of Universal's *The Invisible Man*—has signed on to play Sir John Talbot. Upon reading the script, however, he notices that many of the best lines are spoken by others. Rains thinks Sir John would be better served with those lines for himself.

Waggner, meanwhile, has his own to-do list for Siodmak.

First off, he's *showing* a wolf man on screen. There won't be any of this "imagining" nonsense.

Second, he thinks it would be better if Larry *Gill* became Larry *Talbot*, Sir John's son. If he doesn't sound Welsh, well, that's because he's been away in America for 18 years thanks to a family rift. He only comes back now because his older brother has been killed—and, get this—in a hunt!

Third, Frank won't kill the monster...Sir John will. And with Larry's cane, no less—after trying to prove to his son that this whole werewolf thing *is only in his mind!*

The Wolf Man had been set to go before the cameras on September 8. But with these changes needing to be made, production is pushed back by seven weeks.

* * *

Monday, October 27, 1941. Shooting commences on *The Wolf Man*.[17]

Both producing and directing this time, Waggner has $180,000 to spend. He's got the leftover cathedral set from *The Hunchback of Notre Dame*. He's got an atmospheric Welsh woods, eerily laced with chemical fog. He's got cinematographer Joseph Valentine, who will soon shoot *Saboteur* and *Shadow of a Doubt* for Alfred Hitchcock. He's got Jack Pierce whipping up what will become one of the most recognizable monsters in cinema history. He's got actors Claude Rains, Evelyn Ankers, Bela Lugosi, Maria Ouspenskaya, Ralph Bellamy, and Warren William.

And he's got syndicated columnist Jimmie Fiddler's report in the morning paper:

> "Lon Chaney, Jr. and Universal are having words, his being, 'I want more money and bigger parts'..."

It's as if the ghost of Chaney's stepmom is whispering in his ear, "A man must never settle for less than he is worth."

Meanwhile, as we've seen, Chaney and Evelyn Ankers have already crossed swords. She's managed to placate him for now. But she wonders what might be worse...being his enemy? Or being his friend?

"That was around the time that he was just making a name of his own and exposed to the star treatment," she'll explain years later. "People were always comparing him to his father, who had only died about 10 years previous. I think he was very defensive about that."

To ease boredom and entertain himself, Chaney embarks on a series of practical jokes.

"Lon's attempts at humor, while they probably would have gone over big in a fraternity house, were sometimes not pleasant," Ankers remembers.

So if someone gets doused by a half-filled bucket of water, say, set precariously on a partially opened door, there isn't any doubt who's behind it.

"When he wasn't drinking, he was the sweetest," Ankers says. "Sometimes, he hid it so well that one couldn't be sure."

Meanwhile, Jack Pierce is working out The Wolf Man's makeup design.

"The Wolf Man makeup, though it takes four hours to apply, is not as complicated as the Frankenstein Monster's," Pierce will explain. "It consists principally of an artificial nose piece and bristles on the head, face, and neck, which are literally applied yak hair by yak hair. After the application, I singe the hair to give it that 'animal-like' appearance. I also make-up Chaney's feet and I give him claws."[18]

What Pierce doesn't mention is that the yak hair is augmented with shreds of kelp—seaweed—the smell of which is very unpleasant. He also dresses the Wolf Man in a black shirt and pants.

And although the makeup takes less than an hour to remove, for Chaney, this is the toughest time.

"I'm all hot and itchy and tired, and I've got to sit in that chair for forty-five minutes more while Pierce just about kills me ripping off the stuff he put on in the morning!" he gripes. "Sometimes we take an hour and he leaves *some* of the skin on my face!"

Why not sleep with the makeup on? a reporter asks.

"I'd thought of it," Chaney says, "but I'm afraid my eyes might glue shut overnight."

These discomforts become engrained in Chaney's memory. In 1969, when film historian Gary Dorst asks him to name his most uncomfortable makeup, Chaney almost jumps down his throat:

"Somebody of your age[19] ought to know better," he barks. "The Wolf Man, of course!"

As such, tensions develop between Chaney and Pierce, and the roller coaster ride begins. As a result, when asked years later if he enjoyed working with Chaney, Pierce is taken aback.

"Yes and no," he answers. "That's about all I can say."

Pierce isn't the only one taking heat from the star. According to Siodmak, he's on Chaney's hit list, too.

"Playing that gruesome monster, my friend Lon Chaney Jr. was sitting during lunch break in the studio commissary, but alone," the screenwriter recalls. "In his Wolf Man makeup, he looked so disgusting that nobody would sit with him. He could only feed himself by sucking liquid through a straw."

"If I find the S.O.B. who made up this monster," Chaney growls, "I'm gonna hit him over the head!"

But it's the transformation scenes that really get Chaney's goat.

The Wolf Man transforms in three sequences. Each features lap dissolves—Chaney will be subject to changes in makeup that will be shot on set and blended together in post-production. He's lucky in that Waggner has decided to focus on his feet for the initial two. In the first, Talbot goes from man to beast in five shots, featuring four dissolves. In the second, he reverts from beast to man in four shots, featuring three dissolves.

The climactic transformation focuses on Talbot's face. Here, Chaney endures six changes of makeup.[20] The finished scene features five dissolves.

These scenes are tough on Chaney and the crew. John P. Fulton is responsible for making sure the separate shots will line up. Techs scurry around with tape measures. Anything that can be is secured so there won't be an awkward jump in the completed film.

Chaney, in full harness, is forced to remain prone. Waggner rolls film, then cuts. Chaney's profile is sketched on a sheet of glass mounted in front of the camera. Pierce then removes the makeup and applies the next stage to the actor—in this case, less. The camera operator checks Chaney through the glass—"Your shoulder is up"—then the glass is removed. Waggner rolls more film, cuts, and the process painfully repeats.

These are not Chaney's favorite days.

"He did not appear to be in good humor with all of them fussing about him, with the lighting and makeup changes," Ankers recalls.

In later years, he will—perhaps understandably—exaggerate the agony of shooting these scenes.

When Chaney catches up with Siodmak soon after this ordeal, he half jokes that he's contemplated killing him.

"I'm only a badly-paid writer," Siodmak responds. "I have no influence on the production. All I'm trying to do is collect a few bucks to feed my family."

The makeup does have two very positive perks, however.

First, it's a way of tormenting Ankers, whom he increasingly dislikes.[21]

"I was standing on the set, occupied with learning lines or something like that when I felt a tap on my shoulder," she remembers. "Turning around, expecting to see Ralph Bellamy or one of the other production members, I found myself inches away from a snarling beast! He bared his fangs and grabbed me with these hairy claws. I almost jumped right out of my skin."

Chaney is very amused. Ankers is not.

"Once was enough for me," she says, "but not him."

Second, Chaney realizes that he's creating a unique character all his own. This may be the part that topples his father…

"He knew how much this film could mean to him," film historian Greg Mank will say years later.

"Of course, I believe that *The Wolf Man* is the best of my horror films," Chaney tells Dorst, "because he is *mine!*"

* * *

Like *Man Made Monster*, George Waggner shoots *The Wolf Man* quickly and efficiently.

Unlike *Man Made Monster*, the actors find themselves subject to danger.

To begin with, there is a problem with the bear.

According to Ankers, the bear Larry Talbot is set to fight at the gypsy carnival is 600 pounds, old, and stinks to high Heaven. Though the presence of the bear's trainer is meant to be reassuring, Chaney smells a rat.

He has no problem going toe-to-toe with Broderick Crawford. But his hunter's instincts tell him there's something off about this bear…

"He wouldn't get within 20 feet of the old bear while it was on the set," Ankers says.

This is all well-and-good for Universal; Chaney is known for wanting to do his own stunts, which can be dangerous. Having a double do battle with the bear makes a lot of sense.

But there are scenes leading up to that battle that need to feature the actual leads.

The premise: Talbot, Gwen, and Frank are wandering through the crowded carnival when they spot a gypsy with a bear on a chain.

"Later, Lon was to wrestle the bear when the werewolf personality began to overcome his human side," Ankers explains.

When Ankers passes, the bear apparently sees something he likes…

The cast breaks character. The crew drops their equipment. Suddenly, everyone's running.

Chaney glances behind him. He grabs Ankers by the arm and starts to run as well.

Ankers is completely confused. *Is Chaney pulling another one of his stupid jokes?*

She breaks free of his grip. He keeps running.

And then Ankers turns...

"I am greeted by this great beast," she recalls, "standing on his hind legs, almost seven feet tall!"

She bolts as well. But the bear keeps coming, dragging his trainer behind him.

In an adrenaline-fueled panic, Ankers flies up a ladder. An electrician pulls her onto a lighting scaffold while grips blind the bear with floodlights. The trainer manages to recover and finally gets control of the animal.

"Getting down those wooden scaffolds was a lot harder than it was going up them," Ankers notes.

As planned, when Talbot fights the bear, a double does the rough stuff, while Chaney—not doubt very grateful—appears only in close-ups.[22]

However, Chaney *is* expected to fight another animal on his own when—as Larry Talbot—he beats a werewolf named Bela to death with his silver cane.

In human form, Bela is played—and well—by Bela Lugosi. The star of Universal's *Dracula* (1931) has just turned 59, however, and decently-paid parts are hard to come by. *The Wolf Man* is his first film with Chaney, though it won't be his last.[23]

In werewolf form, Bela is played—and also well—by Moose, a huge German shepherd weighing in at 120 pounds.

"The studio rounded up some dogs it said looked like wolves," Chaney will remember later. "Only they wouldn't wrestle."

Then, the actor comes across Moose, who belongs to a Universal watchman.

"Why not try him?" Chaney suggests.

Shooting the scene, Chaney's hands are protected by sponge rubber covered with thick leather gloves.

"Moose got in there with me and gave me a real fight," Chaney says, "because he was a smart dog and knew what to do."

Still, Moose bites him so hard between the thumb and index finger that Chaney's bones are broken. On film, the fight is very effective.

Always impressed with anyone who can scrap with him and survive, Chaney buys Moose from the watchman, trains him, and rents him out for film parts at $25 a day.

"We fell in love," Chaney will laugh.

Later, Waggner is set to shoot the climactic scene: Gwen is saved from certain death at The Wolf Man's hands in the foggy woods by Larry's father, who unknowingly—and tragically—kills his own son in the process.

The sets are dressed with prop trees from *All Quiet on the Western Front*, *The Black Cat*, and *Son of Frankenstein*; the trees have been painted black and are coated with glycerin. Then, chemical fog is released.

Before long, production designer Robert Boyle has a revelation: "By moving some of these trees—turning them around, really, is what it amounted to—we could get a different set or a different part of the forest with a little bit of a change."

In the finished film, the fog-drenched woods are most impressive. But on set, there's a downside.

The fog can be toxic.

Feature: Ankers as Gwen is chased through the woods and cornered by the vicious Wolf Man. He begins to choke her and she faints.

Suddenly, Sir John appears out of the night and confronts the beast. The Wolf Man drops Gwen on the foggy ground and charges, intending to eliminate the threat.

Ankers has been instructed to stay on the ground until Waggner yells, "Cut!"

She never hears him.

"I had been overcome by the fumes and passed out," she explains. "Fortunately, someone in the crew nearly tripped over me and I was saved."

But the troubles aren't over yet.

The Wolf Man and Sir John engage in battle. It's Chaney and Rains in the close-ups, and stunt doubles in the wide shots.

Always worried about overacting, Rains has instructed Waggner to keep him in check. But at this climactic moment, Sir John is in a fight for his life against a much bigger, stronger adversary. If there's any time to let loose, this is it.

In a moment of frenzy, Rains swings the 10-pound, silver-handled cane wildly...and bashes Chaney in the right eye.

"Chaney came off second best in a fight with Claude Rains, although he out-measured his opponent by 60 pounds and five inches," a Universal press release reports.

In spite of the immediate application of ice packs, Chaney's eye swells up. When he leaves for home, he's got an epic shiner.

Rains is horrified by his actions. He apologizes repeatedly. Chaney tells him to forget it—this ain't the first time he's been hurt, and it won't be the last.

Still, Rains is inconsolable.

"Or maybe," Ankers surmises, "he used his exceptional acting talents and was getting even with Lon for something Lon might have pulled on *him*, too!"

* * *

Tuesday, November 14, 1941. Things are going well enough on *The Wolf Man* that Universal is pleased to make an announcement: Chaney will be the next actor to play Frankenstein's Monster.

Tuesday, November 25, 1941. *The Wolf Man* wraps.

Ted Kent (*Son of Frankenstein*) cuts the picture. Charles Previn, Hans J. Salter, and Frank Skinner work their musical magic. *The Wolf Man* is set for release on December 9.

But before that happens, the world turns upside down.

* * *

Sunday, December 7, 1941. Imperial Japanese forces attack Pearl Harbor. The U.S. Naval Fleet is dealt a stunning blow, and 2,402 Americans lose their lives.

Convinced they're next on the list, California residents panic. They wonder *when*—not *if*—an attack will occur.

Reacting to rumors of Japanese aircraft carriers sighted in the Bay Area, Oakland orders a blackout. Other major cities—including Los Angeles—follow suit.

On December 8, the U.S. declares war on Japan. America is now knee-deep in World War II.

Bunkers are built, anti-aircraft weapons are set up, radio silence is enforced. And people begin wondering exactly what should happen with the Japanese among them…

Always patriotic, and never a fan of "foreigners," Chaney is enraged by the attack. He intends to serve in the Marines as a cook. But a medical exam reveals that he has a heart condition—"a bad ticker," as he puts it. Newspapers report that he's "moving heaven and earth to enlist," but it never happens. He's classified 4-F.

Meanwhile, panic ensues at Universal. Not only is the country at war and the west coast under threat, but they have product to move. Who in their right mind is going to want to see a horror fantasy like *The Wolf Man* amidst the real-life horror of war?

Well, a lot of people, as it turns out.

* * *

Tuesday, December 9. As planned, *The Wolf Man* is released.

While none of the reviews are raves, a number of publications treat the film with respect.

The Hollywood Reporter, for example, likes it.

"Lon Chaney assumes the really terrifying makeup created by Jack P. Pierce and bears favorable comparison to his esteemed father," they note. "And he is pleasantly personable as the untransformed Larry…however, [we] wouldn't dare guess the box office appeal of a horror film previewed the week America went to War."

Variety likes it, too:

"*The Wolf Man* is a compactly-knit tale of its kind, with good direction and performances…but dubious entertainment at this particular time…Young Chaney gives a competent performance both straight and under makeup for the dual role."

The Harrison's Report is also in favor:

"[T]he hero, who becomes infected with the werewolf disease, is a pitiful character for whom one feels sympathy. There are a few scenes that are properly frightening…Not for children."

Other publications—if they don't ignore the film completely—rip it to shreds.

The New York Times, as expected, is vicious:

"[N]obody is going to go on believing in werewolves or Santa Clauses if the custodians of these legends don't tell them with a more convincing imaginative touch...[the Wolf Man] looks a lot less terrifying and not nearly as funny as Mr. Disney's Big, Bad Wolf."

No matter. The picture is a hit—Universal's biggest of the season. Plus, it has aged remarkably well, and critical reassessments beginning in the 1970s treat it as the important work it is.

"The film is as close to tragedy as twentieth-century pop culture would come," Arthur Lennig—Lugosi's biographer—will sum up in 2003.

By May 1942, *The Wolf Man* has made a million bucks—roughly $18 million today, which is great business in pre-blockbuster Hollywood. Chaney is dubbed the studio's new Master Character Creator, and claims that Universal gets more fan mail for him than anyone else.

And his feelings about The Wolf Man?

"He was my baby!"

He's as close to topping his father as he'll ever get.

August 17, 1944

Thursday, August 17, 1944. *The Los Angeles Times*, page 13: "Boy May Adopt Lon Chaneys as His Parents."

The boy is 8-year-old Burrell Lee Howard Devine. He's the youngest of four siblings. His father has been dead since 1941. His stepdad, Jerry Wade, once worked for the Chaneys on their ranch, but has since moved to Stockton. Thanks to a severe housing shortage, Wade's unable to find a place to rent that will allow children. As a result, five members of the family have lived in a one-room apartment for a year. To make matters worse, Wade has recently been injured and is unable to work. His wife brings in what she can as a waitress.

"We just couldn't give Burrell a decent home under those conditions," his mother says.

"We couldn't give Burrell a decent home because of the housing shortage," Wade concurs, "and the Chaneys, who like him, can provide it."

The plan is to give Burrell a year to make sure he's happy with Patsy and Lon.

"You see, we're not adopting Burrell," Chaney explains to *The Times*. "We're hoping that Burrell will see fit to adopt us. The lawyers can phrase the legal side of it in any way they please."

Since *The Wolf Man*'s release, Chaney has appeared in no less than 17 films—he's just completed *The*

Mummy's Curse—and the money's good, so Burrell finds that the creature comforts are enticing.

"A lawn covered with ivy so that it will never need mowing," *The Times* reports. "A fence to climb and a dog to tag along at his heels. A tree so loaded with peaches that only a frame keeps the branches from breaking. Promises of vacations on a ranch with lots of horses. And an assortment of fishing tackle to make any Ike Walton[1] envious."

But wait—there's more…

"When the man next door gets the chickens off the lot, Mr. Chaney may build a swimming pool," Burrell says. "I don't know yet if I'll get homesick."

This isn't the first time the Chaneys have determined to adopt a child. Unable to have kids of their own—and with Lon's sons from his first marriage getting older[2]—adopting has been part of their plan since Chaney's paychecks have become regular.

"I only wish I had enough money to give countless deserving orphans a good home," he'll lament. "The lousiest thing in this world is to grow up without love."

While life with Burrell works out initially, the adoption never happens.

"We had to send him back," Patsy says later. "His mother gave us some trouble."[3]

Saddened, Patsy and Lon determine to continue their efforts.

* * *

Chaney's career whirlwind begins on Monday, December 15, 1941 when cameras start turning on *The Ghost of Frankenstein*. He stars as the Frankenstein Monster, the first actor to follow in Karloff's 13-pound boots.

"It was tough enough with the 'ghost' of Dad floating around Universal," he'll explain in 1971, "but when I had to take over the part of the Frankenstein Mon-ster from Boris Karloff, the pressure was on."

Once again, he finds Jack Pierce's makeup to be a painful ordeal.

"It was almost as bad as *The Wolf Man*...," he says. "But at least I had most of that picture finished without makeup. For *Ghost of Frankenstein*, I had to be in makeup for the total shoot."

On one particular occasion, the Monster's headpiece causes him considerable agony.

"I must have been allergic to the Monster's headpiece or the glue, because I broke out in a rash under that gray-green greasepaint and I started to itch—all down my back and around my forehead and scalp."

Unlike his Pop, *this* Chaney doesn't suffer in silence.

"Hot-tempered, impatient, and a bit arrogant about his newly-won stardom, Chaney proved a trial to Pierce during some sessions," film historian Greg Mank will write in 1981.

With his head and back itching like crazy, Chaney doesn't care how Jack Pierce feels. He wants the headpiece removed. Immediately.

No one acknowledges him.

Enraged, Chaney rips the appliance off himself.

"Part of my forehead came off with it," he ruefully admits.

He stays home for a week to heal.

* * *

While *The Ghost of Frankenstein* doesn't have Karloff, it does have Bela Lugosi, Evelyn Ankers, Lionel Atwill, Ralph Bellamy, and—most surprisingly—Sir Cedric Hardwicke. Directing is Erle C. Kenton (*Island of Lost Souls*).

But Chaney's favorite member of the cast and crew turns out to be 5-year-old actress Janet Ann Gallow.

"I used to watch him get his makeup on in the morning," she'll recall in 2015, "so I knew what he looked like underneath all the makeup. I loved him a lot. He was a great guy."

After the film is done, Gallow will spend time with Lon and Patsy at their home. When her mother dies in 1946, Chaney offers to adopt both Janet and her brother—a plan Janet's father understandably rejects.

With *The Ghost of Frankenstein* in release—and financially successful—Chaney is assigned the part of The Mummy, yet another Karloff role. But while Dear Boris spent only one brief scene in Jack Pierce's wrappings—and had pages of dialogue after—Chaney is wrapped up full-time, and has no lines at all. He'll eventually limp through three mediocre pictures like this, griping all the way.

Columnist Robbin Coons finds him in a particularly foul mood on one Mummy set.

"He's all wound up in dirty rags with a long underwear foundation," Coons observes. "He has a dirty-rag face, too, like a thoroughly embalmed actor. In fact, he looks like anybody else of his size and build all wrapped up, and what is embalmed for the moment is actually his career. You take away an actor's face and what has he left? Frustration."

"I've no lines, no face," Chaney complains. "But I have a bet. I've bet that some day one of these pictures will lose money, and then I won't have to do anymore. So far, though…"

"He didn't like the mask," explains Reginald LeBorg, director of *The Mummy's Ghost* (1944). "After two hours, he became tired, couldn't get his breath, and began to perspire. The suit was pretty uncomfortable."

At one point, openly sipping bourbon on the set of *The Mummy's Curse*, he's called out by director Leslie Goodwin:

"Please don't drink too much before we shoot."

"Why?" Chaney replies, annoyed. "I have no lines and I have to drag my butt through the mud."

This kind of assignment is not going to help him eclipse his father.

The fact that Universal is running him through a series of retreads is one thing. But the role that really miffs the actor is that of *stereotype*. He's all-too-familiar with that one, having lived it as a cowboy, and then big, dumb guys thanks to Lennie.

"Now, I'm typed as an ideal horror-man," he'll say in 1943. "I scare women and children, and give the men shudders."

"Chaney yearns for the Charles Boyer type of roles," studio publicity notes.[4]

He's especially offended when Universal passes on him for the 1943 remake of *The Phantom of the Opera*, which stars Claude Rains instead. What's this all about? The studio is more than happy to exploit his name for profit—after all, starting with *The Wolf Man*, they've been billing him as LON CHANEY against his will—so what are they thinking with *Phantom*? No matter how much he's being paid—and it *is* a considerable amount—slights like these churn up his insecurities. *They don't think they can make money on it with me in Pop's role rather than Rains?* Once again, he's denied a toe-to-toe showdown with his father's ghost.

Next, Universal stars Chaney in six pictures based on a popular book and radio series called *The Inner Sanctum*. Because he'll be portraying intellectuals—doctors, professors, chemists, etc.—there will be no need for heavy makeup.[5]

Artistically, however, the films are a mixed bag, as are Chaney's performances in them. But they make a mint for Universal, and why not? They take about 10 to 12 days to shoot, and cost only $150,000.

Even a choice assignment as Dracula in the atmospheric *Son of Dracula* (1943) turns out to be a double-edged sword. Again, it's somebody else's signature part, and an enraged, offended Bela Lugosi badmouths him. Then, as time passes, film historians review his heft rather than his performance,[6] as if there's some law that says vampires have to be skinny.

So as little Burrell Lee Howard Devine heads back to his mom and stepdad, there are only two things in Chan-ey's professional life that comfort him:

The Wolf Man and alcohol.

* * *

Monday, October 12, 1942. Shooting begins on *Frankenstein Meets the Wolf Man*. Directing is Roy William Neill (*Sherlock Holmes and the Secret Weapon*).

The project actually starts as *The Wolf Man Meets Frankenstein*, since the picture as conceived is a sequel to *The Wolf Man*. Curt Siodmak is given the task of bringing the Titans of Terror together.

This isn't going to be easy.

"The Wolf Man's head had been bashed in by his own father in a Welsh forest," notes *The Saturday Evening Post* on May 23. "Frankenstein's monster had last been seen crushed under huge timbers in a burning house somewhere in the Balkans."

Characteristically, Siodmak is frustrated by the assignment…at first.

"Whipped cream is good and herring is good," he complains, "so they think they should be better together."

But then, he gets a brainwave: The Wolf Man wants to die. The Monster wants to live. What if the secrets in Dr. Frankenstein's notebook can help each of them get what they desire?

Add to this the fact that Chaney is the last guy to have played both parts. This gives producer George Waggner a brainwave of his own.

Why don't we have Chaney play The Wolf Man *and* The Monster in this one? he asks Neill. We can use doubles and stunt men. Think of the publicity!

Neill begins planning. But it turns out the trickery involved will cost too much. Plus, does anybody really want to deal with Chaney in *two* heavy makeups?

As such, The Monster is offered to Bela Lugosi[7]…which makes some sense, in that Lugosi's character's brain was deposited into The Monster's skull at the end of *Ghost*. The part as written for *Meets* portrays The Monster as blind and weak, but able to speak, so Lugosi develops a variation of his Ygor voice for the dialogue.

Meanwhile, Frederick C. Othman, a Hollywood Correspondent for the United Press, catches up with Chaney on the set one fine October day—in full Wolf Man regalia, no less. Hanging with the actor is Moose, who serves as The Wolf Man's stand in.

"This almost seems too good to be true," Chaney tells Othman. "I'm only worrying that maybe people will say that I'm a hoarder. But I can't help it. I still remember those days when my wife and I didn't eat. When I got some money, I bought me hundreds of cans and some apparatus for using them. I've canned food of all kinds. I've gone out in the ocean and caught tuna and canned them. I've shot game and canned it. It makes me feel better to see all that food, because a fellow never can tell how long his luck's going to run in the movies."

It's obvious that trust issues still run deep in Creighton Tull Chaney.

Still, he's on his best behavior during the shoot—even though the Wolf Man makeup has been somewhat expanded.[8] His colleagues take notice.

"Lon Chaney is one of the nicest, sweetest people in the world," says Ilona Massey, the Hungarian-born actress who plays Dr. Frankenstein's daughter. "I never had any difficulty with my co-stars, but Chaney was something special."[9]

Trouble ensues one day when Chaney and Maria Ouspenskaya—reprising her Maleva role from *The Wolf Man*—are thrown from a horse-drawn cart. One of the wheels hits a rut, and the cart capsizes, trapping the actors underneath. Luckily, the horse stops, and Moose leaps into action, guarding Ouspenskaya from the horse's hooves until she can be rescued.[10]

As it turns out, Ouspenskaya and Chaney aren't the only accident victims on the production:

- Script handler Connie Earl gets hit by an ice machine, resulting in a gash on her head.
- Stagehand Jack Ross gets nailed by a falling prop tree.
- Gaffer Max Nippell is knocked unconscious by an improperly secured beam.

It's worse for poor Bela Lugosi. The 40-pound Monster makeup and costume cause him no end of suffering. The 60-year-old actor's energy has been sapped to the point that he's collapsed twice on set already.

The nadir occurs while filming close-ups of the climactic battle with The Wolf Man. In the process, Lugosi goes crashing into a stone wall and is knocked out.

All of this leads gossip columnist Erskine Johnson to ask: is Universal's Phantom Stage—where much of the picture is being shot—jinxed?

Waggner is having none of it, though he acknowledges such rumors "add to the mystery and horror of a horror picture...

"It all started the first week of production when Miss Massey packed her bags and left her husband, Alan Curtis,[11]" Waggner concedes. "Next came a series of illnesses which gave us a headache for a few days, and then Lugosi weakened after losing 15 pounds in three weeks. He can't stand more than a few hours now in makeup. If he can pull through this battle scene, we'll all feel easier."

Off the record, it soon becomes obvious that Bela *won't* be able to pull through this battle scene. Or much of anything else.

But since stunt men Eddie Parker and Gil Perkins are doubling The Monster and The Wolf Man in long shots for the battle anyway, why not just let them take over for Lugosi in other scenes as well?[12]

With this strategy in place, Neill wraps principal photography on November 11.

Edward Curtiss (*Saboteur*) cuts the film. Hans J. Salter does the music, incorporating leitmotifs from both *The Wolf Man* and *The Ghost of Frankenstein*. A preview is set up for the suits.

"All were enjoying Neill's superbly atmospheric direction and Chaney's better-than-usual performance," Greg Mank writes in 1981, "until there came a scene which originally followed Talbot's rescuing of the Monster from the ice."

It's the first scene featuring the talking Lugosi Monster.

Exactly who is to blame for what happens next is uncertain. Siodmak blames Lugosi, whom he claims can't act. Others have blamed Siodmak for writing cringeworthy lines.

No matter. The suits in the screening room are laughing hysterically.

Panicked, Waggner orders Curtiss to cut all of Lugosi's dialogue.

But that's not all.

"To make matters even worse," Mank says, "all references to the Monster's blindness were expunged as well. Hence, Lugosi's stretching and groping mannerisms no longer made any sense. The damage dealt to Lugosi's sincere but weak performance was devastating."[13]

Frankenstein Meets the Wolf Man—sliced and diced second half and all—debuts in Los Angeles on February 18, 1943. *Variety* likes it, *The Hollywood*

Reporter makes fun of it, and *The New York Times* trashes it.

Rightly or wrongly, the suits blame any problems with the film on Lugosi—he won't make a picture at the studio again until 1948.

Chaney, however, comes out of this one with an enhanced reputation. It's one of his best performances, The Wolf Man story has been treated with respect, and the film makes money. If Bela Lugosi is the fall guy, well, there's nothing he can really do about that.

* * *

Alcohol.

After The Wolf Man, it's the subject that's most associated with Lon Chaney, Jr.

Check the testimony:

- "He and Broderick Crawford and Andy Devine were all pals and they used to get together and do a lot of drinking. When we went on location to Big Bear, the three of them didn't have to worry about keeping warm. If they weren't beating the hell out of each other, they drank enough to generate enough heat to keep us all warm." – Producer Paul Malvern
- "I'm not a drinker. And he invited me to sit and drink, and I could sit a little bit but that's all. And

he invited me home to meet his wife and drink. And I couldn't do it." –Director Reginald LeBorg
- "Chaney's drinking meant that his performance became variable after lunch. He was not a closet drinker, however. To the contrary, as early as 1942 he freely advised directors to get what they could from him before one p.m." –Writer David J. Hogan
- "Lon Chaney—well, he drank too much and I think it killed him in the end…Chaney was a sweet guy, provided he knew where he was at the moment." –Producer Aubrey Schenck
- "Yes, he did drink heavily. This problem meant that we had to make sure that his dialogue scenes were completed by lunch time…in the evenings, he bordered on the incoherent…the overwhelming impression was of a sad and lonely man." –Director Don Sharp
- "Lon Chaney, Jr. had a briefcase full of booze, and was drunk more or less the whole time." –Script supervisor Renee Glynne
- "He brought a bottle of vodka around with him all the time and drank from it before he went onto the set." –Actor David Weston
- "He was an alcoholic at the time, but since he wanted so badly to do a good job on this film, he made a truly heroic effort to stay on the wagon during the shoot, allowing himself only one glass of beer in mid-afternoon in order to get through the day." –Director Jack Hill
- "Why they had him as a star is beyond me. He was roaring drunk!" –Actor Martin Kosleck

- "We had a case of booze as we drove up to his ranch—a seven-or-eight-hour drive—and we drank like crazy…we had to get up early, about two or three in the morning, to go hunting. Lon shook me and woke me up, and in his hand, he was holding a glass…I took a sip and choked—it was straight booze! *That* was an eye-opener!" – Actor Peter Coe
- "Lon Chaney was a darling, darling man—but drunk as a skunk!" –Actress Gloria Talbott

And so on.

Prone to depression, Chaney—like many famous actors, writers, artists, and musicians—self-medicates. Often, the booze is the oil that greases the gears of good times and helps ensure sleep.

But by the mid-1940s, it begins to turn on him…sometimes in public.

For example:

It's 1944. Boris Karloff is back in California—he's been a success on Broadway as Jonathan Brewster in *Arsenic and Old Lace*. When Karloff signs a two-picture deal, Universal invites the press to a dinner party designed to show off their stable of world-class horror stars: Karloff, Chaney, Lugosi, and George Zucco.

Take *that*, Val Lewton!

Also invited is Evelyn Ankers and her husband, actor Richard Denning, who has recently joined the U.S. Navy.[14] Some genius seats the Chaneys next to them.

Chaney's drinking. But it's not helping his mood tonight.

Maybe he's aggravated because the studio's making a fuss over Karloff. Maybe he's not happy being in the same room with Lugosi. Or maybe he isn't thrilled by having to spend the evening sitting next to Ankers.

Whatever the case may be, he begins making what Ankers calls "rude, uncalled-for remarks" toward Denning.

Denning ignores him. But Chaney pushes it:

"How come you're in the Navy and still in Los Angeles?"

He has Denning's attention now.

"It's a lot better than *not* being in the service at all during wartime," Denning fires back.

This touches a nerve—Chaney's tried to join the Marines, but has been turned down. He smolders.

Dessert is served: coffee and pistachio ice cream.

"I've got a little ice cream on my sleeve," Chaney says.

He wipes it on Denning's uniform.

Denning picks up his ice cream and smashes it into Chaney's face.

"He looked as if he were back in makeup for one of his monster characters," Ankers cracks later.

Enraged, Chaney picks up his coffee, intending to fling it at Denning. But somehow, Ankers manages to step in and calm him down.

"Then," Ankers recalls, "we all had to troop in the next room to have our pictures taken!"

The unhappy suits take note.

* * *

March, 1943. Pittsburgh, Pennsylvania.

Chaney—ever the patriot—is on tour with other Hollywood actors, selling war bonds. Columnist Kaspar Monahan catches up with him.

"Lon Chaney, Jr., I mean, is the sort of citizen it's best to have on your side in case of a free-for-all brawl," Monahan writes. "He towers upward six feet three and a half inches,[15] weighs 225 pounds, and his shoulders are so wide he has to turn sidewise to go through an ordinary doorway."

Monahan finds Chaney in a good mood.

"He's a courteous gent, easy to talk to, no put-on," Monahan notes, "and who doesn't expect folks to kowtow to him because of his famous sire."

"Dad, after all, was his own makeup man," Chaney says. "He was the boss. Now, I have to let makeup men do what they will to me, and, brother, what they do to me! Mind now, I'm not squawking; I like my work, but there are times when I think I just can't stand it."

The tour is successful, Chaney says, and he enjoys being a part of it. He also observes that selling bonds is easy compared to a day in Hollywood.

"Easy?" Monahan asks, rhetorically. "He collapsed at one town on tour. For all his size, he's a bundle of nerves. And is heart—his 'ticker' as he calls it—isn't so good."

Regarding the future, Chaney and Monahan agree that it would be nice to see the actor doing substantial parts in prestigious pictures, as he did with Lennie—in stature, if not in type.

"The big guy's sensitive. Yeah—and shy, and I'm not kidding," Monahan concludes. "I like him both as a man and an actor."

* * *

In an attempt to combine business with pleasure, Chaney intends to see family and friends while selling bonds on the east coast. Up first: his sister-in-law, a W.A.C.C. stationed in Hartford, Connecticut.

When he gets there, he learns she's on leave—she's getting married in California.

Up next: his brother-in-law, stationed in Pensacola, Florida.

When he gets there, he learns the man's been transferred to Philadelphia.

Last but not least: Brod Crawford, now in the Air Force and training in Atlantic City, New Jersey.

When Chaney gets there, he learns Crawford's been reassigned…to Hartford.

Back at the studio, Chaney chats with four visiting sailors, each of whom has been blinded in action at Guadalcanal. All are guided by seeing-eye dogs. Moved by their positive attitudes, Chaney promises to gift their dog trainer with a litter of German shepherd pups.

Sadly, not all dog-related events are so positive. Working on a new picture with Moose, Chaney is devastated when his companion is accidentally killed by an automobile.

"On the day Moose died," reports *Daily Press*, "the entire company in the film in which Chaney and the dog were working observed a full minute of silence out of respect for the beloved animal."

August 19, 1943. *The Los Angeles Times* announces the death of Ralph L. Hinckley, Chaney's former father-in-law and grandfather to Lon Ralph and Ron. Tragically, Hinckley's life is cut off when he's thrown from a horse in Griffith Park.

Chaney's losses continue to mount.

* * *

August 23, 1943. Production begins on *The Mummy's Ghost*. Directing is Reginald LeBorg.

"I really admired your father," LeBorg tells Chaney upon meeting the actor. "You practically emulate him."

"Emulate?" Chaney responds. "I want to top him!"

"You're tremendously talented in your own right," LeBorg says. "You've unquestionably demonstrated that as Lennie and The Wolf Man."

"We'll do something great together, Pappy," Chaney grins, slapping LeBorg on the shoulder.

The dream is still alive.

But while Chaney takes an instant liking to *him*, LeBorg is more reserved.

"At the beginning, Chaney thought I would be his pal," LeBorg explains.

This is not going to happen. To begin with, LeBorg isn't much of a drinker. Plus, LeBorg senses that Chaney needs a father figure, something the director is definitely not comfortable with.

"I was but a few years older than Lon," he points out.

When—after four films together—LeBorg decides he'd like to try directing a musical, Chaney takes it personally.

"You traitor," he says, poking his finger in LeBorg's chest. "We were supposed to do big things together."

"We'll get together again, don't worry."

"I've heard that story before," Chaney fires back, fuming.

The betrayals continue to mount as well...at least, in Chaney's mind.

It'll be the mid-1950s before they'll work on the same movie set again.

* * *

Monday, April 3, 1944. Production begins on *The Devil's Brood*. When it's released in December, it will be known as *House of Frankenstein*.

The picture features Dracula, The Wolf Man, and Frankenstein's Monster. In addition, there is a mad scientist (Karloff) and a hunchbacked henchman (J. Carrol Naish).

There's also a pretty gypsy girl named Ilonka, played by 18-year-old Elena Verdugo.

Curt Siodmak has come up with the story. Edward T. Lowe has written the script. Directing is *Ghost*'s Erle C. Kenton.

Chaney is, of course, The Wolf Man. And once again, Jack Pierce has expanded the makeup. In this film, the beast will be hairier than ever.[16]

"I've played both Frankenstein's monster and the Wolf Man before," he tells Virginia MacPherson of the United Press. "And for my money, I'd rather be a monster. That green goo is mere cold cream compared to the fangs and false hair I get myself messed up with."

The $10,000 flat fee Chaney gets for playing the part—just shy of $150,000 at this writing—takes some of the sting out of the itch.

Interestingly, Chaney claims that his doctor is advising him to alternate parts in horror pictures with comedic roles.

"The reason is not entirely the danger of developing a neurosis," writes columnist Harrison Carroll. "It also has to do with the difficult makeup in the horror films which keep the star from eating properly or even from relaxing in a chair."

At least Chaney *has* a role in *The Devil's Brood*.

Tellingly, Bela Lugosi isn't playing Dracula. That part goes to John Carradine (*The Grapes of Wrath*). Lugosi hasn't been asked to reprise Frankenstein's creation, either.

Even Karloff wants no part of his Dear Old Monster anymore.

"You other guys can have that paint and goo and fangs," he decrees.

Therefore, under the green goo here is 6'4" Glenn Strange. The craggy-faced but genial 220-pound actor has appeared in more than 100 films since 1930, mostly bit parts in Westerns. He also has some monster cred, appearing as a werewolf in PRC's *The Mad Monster* with George Zucco in 1942.

Jack Pierce finds Strange to be an ideal colleague. He looks like a young Karloff, he doesn't need muscle padding, and he's not a complainer.

"This getup is pretty comfortable," Strange tells MacPherson. "The only part that bothers me is the paper eyelids. They usually get in my way when I blink. And the 25-pound shoes slow me down a little."

Producer Paul Malvern is pleased with Strange as well. Strange doesn't need a stunt man. Plus, Strange is cognizant of the fact that he's playing Karloff's signature role in front of Karloff himself. As such, he asks for—and receives—Dear Boris' suggestions on the character's movements and facial expressions.

The set of *The Devil's Brood* is a happy one. When he isn't in front of the camera, Chaney cooks hearty lunches—roast beef, ham hocks and beans, etc.—for his fellow actors. Then—along with Karloff and Naish—he plans a surprise 19th birthday party for Verdugo. Karloff gifts her with a volume of fairy tales by Hans Christian Anderson, while Strange sings

"Happy Birthday" to her in full costume between mouthfuls of cake.

Once again—perhaps because he loves his Wolf Man—Chaney is on his best behavior. His co-stars certainly seem to like him.

"He was a nice guy—a big, good-natured slob," Carradine will remember years later. "He was a pro who knew his business."

"Lon Chaney was a lovely, friendly man," gushes Elena Verdugo.

Of course, there is the day Verdugo and Chaney shoot their mutual death scene—The Wolf Man manages to get a fatal bite in just as Ilonka caps him with a silver bullet.

According to Verdugo, she had yet to see Chaney in makeup. When he leaps at her as the film rolls, she screams to high Heaven.

There will be no need for overdubbing.

* * *

Given how busy Universal keeps him—and how much of his day is spent in varied stages of drunkenness—it's amazing the number of other projects Chaney involves himself with.

One of his most beloved diversions is his ranch.

Chaney hears about the 1300-acre cattle spread—located in Cool, California, about 40 miles north of Sacramento—from his Uncle George. It's a seven-hour drive from the Chaney's home in Los Angeles.

Owned by the Robert S. Jerrett family for nearly 100 years, it features an 80-year-old ranch house. Chaney initially names the property *Lo Cazador* (The Hunstman), but quickly changes it to something more personal: Lennie's Ranch. His plans include expanding upon the 160 head of cow that reside there already and mining gold. He also intends to build guest houses to board the friends who had helped him make his start in The Biz.[17]

An even more ambitious plan involves helicopters.

Something tells Chaney that Hollywood folks would love a 10-minute "air taxi" service from the studios to Malibu. He makes plans with Brian Donlevy, actor and mayor of the Malibu Beach colony, and secures investors—writer John Grant, director Jean Yarborough, and actor Noah Beery, Jr. among them. He also tests Army helicopters at Hamilton Field. After the war is over, he plans to create a six-copter fleet and run the service hourly. All he needs is approval from the Civil Aeronautics Commission.

* * *

Thursday, May 11, 1944. John Jeske, 55, is dead, the victim of a heart attack.

Chaney makes no public comment, but can his thoughts be anything other than *good riddance*?

Jeske's death doesn't relieve a streak of bad luck for the Chaney family, however.

To begin with, the house up at Lennie's Ranch burns down, taking their livestock feed with it.

Then, the 16-year-old son of his caretaker in Cool spends a month in the hospital after falling out of a wagon. The bill comes to $753.16. Highland General Hospital expects Chaney to cough up $500 of that.[18]

Soon after, Lon accidentally sinks a jackknife into his leg while playing a game of Mumbley Peg with one of his sons.

But the capper comes in December, when Patsy needs stitches.

It seems that she's been bitten in the throat by the family parrot.

* * *

September, 1945. Production is humming along on *The Wolf Man vs. Dracula*, which will hit theaters as *House of Dracula* on December 7. Once again, the script is by Ed Lowe, and Erle Kenton is directing.

Glenn Strange and John Carradine from *House of Frankenstein* are back, along with Martha O'Driscoll, Jane Adams, and Onslow Stevens.

Stevens—playing a brilliant and kind-hearted doctor who becomes homicidal when infected by Dracula's blood—will get most of the acting accolades when the film is discussed in years to come.

Chaney is back as Larry Talbot, annoyed that Universal has asked him to postpone a hunting trip with Strange to Colorado—"Too many nimrods getting shot there this season," notes columnist Harrison Carroll.

Things are different in front of the camera. Slimmed down and sporting a mustache,[19] Chaney is featured in print advertisements for Schaefer beer: "Finest beer I ever tasted!" This is the very definition of "expert testimony."

More surprisingly, Chaney actually turns out to be the hero in the new film.

"In all the others, I'm the dirty dog who sprouts fangs during the full moon," he tells Virginia MacPherson. "But somewhere along the middle of this one, they operate on me and presto—I'm a good Joe."

But before he "gets the girl, kills off the other goons, and saves the day"—as MacPherson puts it—there are still two Wolf Man scenes to do, both featuring transformations involving eight stages of makeup.

This proves to be a challenge, given that yak hair shipments from Central Asia have been suspended during the war—and an expected shipment from Chungking after the guns have ceased fire doesn't arrive.

As a result, the beast is not as hairy as he was in *House of Frankenstein*.[20]

Plus, Talbot's cure begs the question: is this it for The Wolf Man?

If so, it seems that Chaney doesn't mind.

"[W]e monsters are really in a rut," he tells writer Arthur Millier. "Instead of dreaming up new ones, they keep bringing the old ones back to life."

What would Chaney like to see?

"Well, for instance, a hairless monster—completely hairless. I can't describe him yet, but he's as hairless as a Mexican dog."

According to Chaney, the screen lacks actual monsters.

"Since my dad's death, there have been characters but no monsters," he says. "A character is something a writer can create in words. A monster is a visual creation—the actor conceives him, and he's born with the aid of a clever makeup man."

Still, when columnist Bob Thomas asks him which of his characters is his favorite, he's loyal to his baby.

"That's easy—the Wolf Man. That's about the only one I can halfway believe in. It's a horror part, and yet it has some sympathy to it. That seems to be the one the kids like best, and that's good enough for me."

Any psychological reactions to playing horror roles?

"Naw. The only thing I do is to wait a half-hour after taking off the makeup before going home...I feel so damn mean by that time of day. I don't want the family to suffer."

Sadly, the family suffers for a different reason when Flora Beck—Patsy's mother—dies on October 20. Her funeral is held on Tuesday, October 23.

Flora's death is but one example of the almost constant stream of bad luck that plagues the Chaneys in 1945.

First, a flood at Lennie's Ranch wipes out the retaining walls for their water supply and wrecks a mile of fencing.

Then, Lon and Patsy are almost arrested when neighbors complain about "ghoulish laughter, screams for mercy, and the slamming of doors"[21] coming from their house. Turns out they're recording horror stories on records to entertain friends.

Next, a fire breaks out in their Hollywood home when a guest accidentally ignites a shower curtain with a gas heater. The damages are estimated at $600.

Then Lon Ralph—now 17, and a solid six-footer[22]—breaks his leg playing football for Hollywood High.

Next, Hallock Chaney—cousin to the late Lon, Sr.—visits Lon Jr. in Hollywood…and promptly disappears.[23]

And finally, when the Chaneys advertise that their guest house is for rent, they're so overwhelmed by the response that they have to ditch town.

"Every time Lon Chaney plays The Wolf Man, some disaster befalls," Harrison Carroll writes.

Still, Lon and Patsy are happy enough to renew their wedding vows. The ceremony is held at 11 PM on Christmas Eve in front of a small group of friends. Lon replaces Patsy's six-dollar silver ring with a five-carat diamond. Judge Cecil D. Holland officiates.

On Christmas day, the Chaneys are off to Mexico with his aunt, uncle, and sons.

Sadly, as 1946 dawns, things take a turn for the worse.

Chaney is dropped by Universal.

This is a betrayal that can mean financial disaster as well.

* * *

Rejoining the uncertain world of freelance actors is a scary prospect as Chaney turns 40. True, life at Universal was often annoying, but the pay was good. And regular. It sticks in his craw that they've let him go. Eventually, he joins an informal club called The KOBUIs—"Kissed off by Universal-International." The founder is Andy Devine, and membership includes Robert Paige, Peggy Ryan, and Rod Cameron.[24]

Publicly, however, Patsy, says her husband welcomes the change.

"He wanted to work at other studios," she'll claim years later.

But—given his rep for being outspoken and drinking heavily on the set—will other studios want to work with *him?*

As it turns out, Paramount is willing to take a chance, but only in comedies.

"The plan is to turn the son of the horror king into a top comedian," columnist Louella Parsons reports in July, "and his first job will be helping Bob Hope supply the laughs in *My Favorite Brunette*...It is unusual for an actor to change so radically his screen characterization as Lon Jr. is doing. It may take more than one picture to stop the kids from squealing with terror when he appears on the screen, but Lon welcomes the change and the chance. He once told me he thought it was a big mistake to try to cash in on his father's reputation."

Still, Chaney figures Universal will come calling again.

"Someday, they're going to need a goon," he tells Bob Thomas, "and they'll have to send for me."

Why you? Thomas asks.

"I'm the only horror man left who can stand the long hours and tortuous makeup," he explains. "The others are on the other side of 40 now. So am I, but I'm crazy enough to take it."

It will be two years before Universal summons him.

Meanwhile, bad luck continues to jinx the family.

In January, Chaney's a passenger on a plane that loses a wing while landing in Nogales. It's a close call.

In February, he faces a lawsuit stemming from the accident on Lennie's Ranch in 1944. The hospital wants $750 now.

In August, Patsy comes down with a bad case of undulant fever.[25] A telephone is installed in Chaney's dressing room at Paramount in case of an emergency. Chaney, meanwhile, is struggling with an eye allergy and is under medical care himself.

In November, William Bush dies.[26]

The beginning of 1947 isn't much better.

In January, Chaney suffers a split lip, cuts on his cheek and hands, and bruises while shooting a fight scene with Randolph Scott for *Albuquerque*. According to columnists Reba and Bonnie Churchill, Lon takes 33 falls and 47 punches in the picture. Offscreen, he wins over the actresses on set by bringing them posies from his garden.

Also in January, he and Patsy are left with a huge hole in their yard when a contractor they've hired to build them a swimming pool is arrested. It turns out C. Dudley Stillwell never properly registered as a contractor, nor did he secure a permit for the work. Chaney loses an $1800 down payment, plus a $500 barn Stillwell has already completed is torn down. Chaney and his lawyer file a suit for $9800 in damages.

The very unhappy actor is pictured in newspapers sitting in the hole, a shovel slung over his shoulder.

Something has to give.

February 5, 1948

It's a wet Thursday morning in Los Angeles, but nobody's complaining. Overnight, soaking rains have finally broken what *The Los Angeles Times* describes as "Southern California's worst drouth in 70 years."

Lon Chaney, Jr. has suffered a drouth as well. From 1941 through 1945, he'd averaged six-to-seven screen appearances per year. But that's when he was with Universal.

Since then, his proposed career as a comedian at Paramount hasn't worked out. As a result, he's subsequently appeared in only three films.

The fact that he's recently been featured in a syndicated, comic-book style newspaper ad for Trim Hair Tonic—tied to his appearance in *Albuquerque*—is small comfort.[1]

Given the limited offers, it's no surprise that he and *Wolf Man* writer Curt Siodmak are forging a plan for their own production company—one that will focus on horror films.

"The Valleyite, who will also star in the pictures, hopes to develop several new monsters that will top even Frankenstein," *The Valley Times* reports.

One potential character? The Lizard Man.

With production beginning on *The Brain of Frankenstein*, Chaney can't help having mixed feelings. On the plus side, he'll be playing Larry Talbot—billed this time as The Wolfman—again. And the money's certainly better than he's been getting for stage revivals of *Born Yesterday* or *Of Mice and Men*.

There's also the fact that Jack Pierce—never a Chaney favorite—has been canned. Bud Westmore runs the makeup department now, and he's cut Chaney's time in the chair to only an hour by creating a foam rubber Wolfman mask that his assistant Emile LaVigne will apply.

But there are downsides, too. Chaney is still pissed at Universal for cutting him loose. He can only take pleasure in the fact that new production chief William Goetz—Louis B. Mayer's son-in-law—has nearly bankrupted Universal-International by insisting on making highbrow pictures.

And then there's Abbott and Costello.

Chaney knows the boys. He'd done a supporting role in *Here Come the Co-Eds* with them back in 1945, and he'd enjoyed the experience. But he's not a fan of slapstick in general, preferring Bob Hope's comic stylings. So even though the script as written treats his character straight, he's not sure how The Wolfman will fare going up against Costello's penchant for outrageous improvisation.

"We monsters should get together and form a union," he'd said back in 1944. "The public comes to see us in a fantastic ghost, or mummy, or zombie, or Frankenstein, or Wolf Man picture, and we expect the audience to take us seriously. Thus far, they have. But now what can we expect when we let ourselves be cast in roles where the horror pictures are spoofed?"

He's not the only one who's wary.

Goetz, for example, absolutely hates Abbott and Costello. And much of his animosity toward them is well deserved.

Bud Abbott and Lou Costello have been a team since 1936. Massive success on stage and in radio results in a movie contract with Universal. Their first starring film, *Buck Privates*, is made for $180,000 in 1941—the exact same cost as *The Wolf Man*.

Studio suits were beside themselves with joy when *The Wolf Man* made its first million.

Buck Privates rakes in $10 million.

Perplexed but giddy, Universal squeezes as many movies out of the team as it can. By the time they start *The Brain of Frankenstein*, they've got 21 features behind them.

Only Costello's 1943 battle with rheumatic heart fever—and the accidental drowning of his infant son, Butch, in November of that year—puts the brakes on their whirlwind schedule.

"It's slow in Hollywood," goes the joke. "Abbott and Costello haven't made a picture all day!"

By 1948, however, the team isn't the cash machine it once was.

Plus, there are the boys themselves. They can be a big-time pain in the ass.

William "Bud" Abbott, 52, comes from a long line of theatrical folks. Offscreen, he's a quiet man but a sharp dresser. He smokes his cigarettes out of a holder. He gambles habitually and loses stacks of cash. He can't remember anybody's name, so he calls everybody "Neighbor."

He also lives in deathly fear of his epilepsy.

His fits are terrible when they hit. He starts drinking by late afternoon to help him cope. This ensures that he's done working when the evening comes.

"Nothing's funny after five o'clock," is his mantra.

Costello, born Louis Francis Cristillo, will turn 42 on March 6. Offscreen, he's a five-foot-four, 200-pound, cigar-chomping ball of fire. His temper tantrums are legendary. The death of his son has made them even worse.

Like Abbott, Costello is native of New Jersey. Also like Abbott, Costello is a habitual gambler. Unlike Abbott, Costello is a poor loser. In spite of the fact that the team makes more than $100 grand per film—and Costello gets sixty percent of it[2]—Lou is constantly broke and hungry for money.

Add the fact that Abbott and Costello's film sets are like a zoo. When they aren't fighting with each other, they're wreaking havoc on their co-stars, Evelyn Ankers among them. While shooting *Hold That Ghost* (1941), they decree that Ankers is "stuffy"—and gift her with a suitcase filled with Kotex.

"I was always glad to find a wall to stand against, or a chair to sit in between takes," she'll recall years later.

Their pranks aren't limited to co-stars. *Hold That Ghost* director Arthur Lubin is horrified when Bud and Lou show him photographs of their wives—both had been strippers, and the photos depict the ladies in the nude.

The Brain of Frankenstein is developed by producer Robert Arthur. The 38-year-old former screen-writer has already worked with the comedy team on *Buck Privates Come Home* (1947) and *The Wistful Widow of Wagon Gap* (1947). He's witnessed the wars between Abbott, Costello, and Goetz. The current skirmish involves bigger budgets for their films. There's no way in Hell that Goetz and his associate Leo Spitz are going to approve. When Costello demands that he and Abbott be paid $25,000 more per film, Goetz suspends them.

Meanwhile, the budget for their new project is locked at $750,000.

But what, exactly, will that new project be?

While chatting with a couple of writers, Arthur has a brainwave: what about pairing up Abbott and Costello with the Frankenstein Monster?

"That's the greatest idea for a comedy that ever was!" says screenwriter Robert Lees.

Arthur, Lees, and Frederic Rinaldo eventually develop the hook: The Monster is getting too smart. A mad scientist decides he needs to dumb the creature down. Costello's screen persona—that of a naïve child-man—makes his brain the perfect solution!

What about Dracula? adds one of the writers, probably remembering monster rallies like *House of Dracula*. What if he had possession of The Monster?

"And why not have The Wolfman to warn the boys?" suggests another.

They decide to toss in The Mummy, The Son of Dracula, and The Invisible Man as well.

The plan is set. Screenwriter Oscar Brodney (*Mexican Hayride, Harvey*) does up a draft, followed by Bertram Millhauser (*Sherlock Holmes Faces Death*). Finally, Lees and Rinaldo, who have been writing Abbott and Costello pictures off and on since *Hold That Ghost*, team up. They pass their draft on to John Grant, A&C's longtime joke-meister.³

Meanwhile, Arthur assembles the cast. He gets Chaney as The Wolfman. He secures Glenn Strange once again for The Monster. And he brings Bela Lugosi back to Universal for the first time since *Frankenstein Meets the Wolf Man* as Dracula.

Rounding out the cast are Lenore Aubert, 34, and *Cat People's* Jane Randolph, 33, both of whom are playing women who fake romantic interest in Costello's character to achieve their (opposite) ends.

But problems occur almost immediately.

To begin with, Goetz doesn't want to read the finished script.

"I don't think those guys are funny," he tells Arthur. "If I read the script, I might not think that *it* was funny, and anything I say might harm your picture. Good luck and God bless you."

Costello, on the other hand, *does* read the script.

He hates it.

"You don't think I'll do that crap, do you?" he explodes. "My five-year old daughter can write something better than that!"

Arthur is taken aback. First of all, he's never known Costello to have ever read a script before. Secondly, he's sure he has a hit on his hands…if he can get the comic to play in it.

"You do the picture," Arthur responds, "and I'll pay you fifty thousand dollars cash for your share of the profits."

"Fifty G's right now?"

"Right now."

Costello is on board…temporarily.

* * *

Friday, February 13, 1948. Chaney finally secures the Placerville properties that John Jeske had inherited from Hazel. This includes his father's prize ranch home.

It has been a long process.

Unable to pay the property taxes, Jeske loses the land to the State of California in 1942. Chaney and his attorney Barry Woodmansee attempt to grab it then, but red tape slows down the purchase.

By 1947, with Jeske dead more than three years, Woodmansee has brokered a deal. All Chaney has to do is pay the back taxes. He does so on August 1, 1947 through the Lon Chaney Estate. To secure the title, Woodmansee probates Jeske's estate.

For Chaney, the taste of this victory over his old enemy is sweet. And the ranch house will become his favorite escape hatch.

* * *

Saturday, February 14, 1948. Bela Lugosi, 65, is on set at Universal-International as Dracula.

Lugosi's hair is darkened, his lips are painted, and his face is caked with powder. He's just postponed a London stage revival of *Dracula* to be here because the $8000 he'll be paid by the studio is much better money. And he desperately needs money. To that end, he's hoping to convince the producers to make at least two more Dracula films.

"There is enough material in the original novel for half a dozen pictures," he asserts.

"He was quite a gentleman," co-star Jane Randolph will say. "He really liked doing Dracula. He did not hint that he felt trapped by the character. He seemed proud of it."

He's about to deliver one of his greatest performances. But subsequent Lugosi/Dracula films will never materialize.

Directing the picture is Charles T. Barton. The five-foot-two, 45-year-old Sacramento native is working on his fifth Abbott and Costello production. His main appeal for Universal-International is that he gets along with Costello.

"A lot of people showed fear, and that's what he loved, so he'd walk all over them," Barton will tell Greg Mank about Costello years later. "But for some reason, with me—and I don't know why in the hell it was—we got along even better than brothers."

Barton is no stranger to Chaney, either. He had directed Chaney in *Rose Bowl* back in 1936. Conceding that Chaney was "a Frankenstein when he was on the bottle," he'll describe the actor's behavior on *The Brain of Frankenstein* in this manner:

> "Lon junior was as gentle as a little lamb—now I'm talking about with *me*. He was so kind—he'd do anything. He was really cooperative. Of course, he had that drinking problem…oh God, *awful*. By late afternoon, he didn't know where he was. He had the problem all through his life, even when he was very young. I don't know why. I guess *he* knew."

This being an Abbott and Costello set, things are typically chaotic.

There's Abbott and Costello's paid jester Bobby Barber, bringing in pies to throw and getting eggs cracked on his bald head. The diminutive, shifty-eyed actor even scores a bit part in the film as a waiter.

Then, there's Costello's refusal to learn his lines from a script he still dislikes.

"He just wanted to stand up and do routines," Barton explains.

Several bits of business from Grant ameliorate Costello's concerns a little, though Lees and Rinaldo feel such things don't belong in the script.

"Grant was a problem for us," Lees will remember in 2008. "After we'd work very hard to get a story together, Grant would come in with something and they'd put it in just because it was from Grant."

These fly-by-the-seat-of-your-pants antics don't sit well with Lugosi. Initially amused, Lugosi's tolerance erodes as takes are blown and time is wasted.

"There were times when I thought Bela was going to have a stroke on the set," Barton remembers. "You have to understand that working with two zanies like Abbott and Costello was not the normal Hollywood set. They never went by the script."

Lugosi handles the situation by glaring at the offenders in his inimitable way.

"We should not be playing while we are working," he'll intone more than once.

Not that it does any good.

Abbott—who generally takes his cues from Costello—isn't in a good mood, either. Arriving on the set from vacation with three broken ribs—he's been tossed by a horse in Phoenix—Bud's more than happy to participate in card games that eat up two or three production days.

"Be there in a minute, Neighbor," he'll respond when called to work, though he has absolutely no intention of following through.

Lou is typically less polite: "Get lost."

There are moments of levity. Strange can't help but laugh while shooting scenes with Costello, encouraging more ad-libs from the already off-script comic. And one fine day, the exotic Aubert puts Strange—in full makeup—on a leash for a walk outside, accompanied by Abbott, Costello, and Chaney…also in full makeup, much to the shock and delight of tourists.

"It was fun," Randolph remembers. "Abbott and Costello were very funny every day, and they were always nice to me...A lot of the crew worked with them before, so they were used to them."

But more typical are the times when the comics go home for the night...and don't return until what feels like days later. As a result, the film will take a week longer than scheduled, costing $33,000 more.

"All three of the 'monsters' were the nicest," Barton will say. "The *real* monsters were Abbott and Costello!"

For his part, Chaney is mostly enjoying the shoot. Bud Abbott's niece Betty remembers him lurking in his dressing room, hoping to pounce on some unsuspecting victim in the same way he tormented Evelyn Ankers.

Sure, Lugosi is cool to him, decreeing that Chaney's drinking on the set is unprofessional, and still nursing a grudge over Lon's casting as the vampire in *Son of Dracula*.[4] But Chaney gets even with him by sarcastically calling him "Pop."

Then, Westmore's Wolfman makeup is certainly more comfortable to wear—a definite improvement over Pierce's approach, which Chaney claims has scarred his face. The streamlined process and added comfort are especially important, given that there are four Wolfman scenes in the script—the most ever.

True, Chaney complains to the press that he loses eight pounds a day because he can't eat with the mask on, but acknowledges that he gains most of it back at dinner. But the transformation sequences still take forever; a full-on barefaced-to-hirsute scene requires six makeup changes and 14 hours—mercifully done over two shooting days on Stage Six.[5] When not in full Wolfman mode, Lon is free to join the pie fights and the other antics.

* * *

Monday, March 15, 1948. Glenn Strange breaks his ankle.

Like Chaney, Strange has benefitted from Westmore's simplified makeup approach. Getting full-on Frankenstein Monster now takes only about an hour. Westmore's even made the footwear more palatable—the Monster's former 13-pound asphalt spreader boots have been replaced by 4-inch elevators made of cork. While the actor is grateful for the comfort, the new boots are awkward—he's tripped over cables more than once.

He's tossing Aubert's stunt double Helen Thurston out of a laboratory window when Thurston's safety wire malfunctions; she suddenly comes swinging right back at him. Attempting to catch her, Strange trips in his cork boots…and just like that, the production is about to lose three more days.

That is, until Chaney hears.

"I'll put the makeup on," he offers. "I'll do it."

"Just as happy as he could be to do it," Barton beams.

Chaney suits up the very next day, throws Thurston through the window, and earns the gratitude of everyone concerned.[6]

Still, he has nagging doubts about how the film is utilizing The Wolfman.

To begin with, Chaney notices that Strange's Monster is treated with dignity. Any laughs Strange generates are generally due to the comic reactions surrounding him.

And Dracula, too, is treated with care. The script includes ripe lines that are delivered by Lugosi with just the right ironic touch.

"There is no burlesque for me," Lugosi will explain. "All I have to do is frighten the boys, a perfectly appropriate activity. My trademark will be unblemished."

But there *is* burlesque for The Wolfman.

As previously noted, there are four Wolfman sequences in the picture. The first—wherein The Wolfman rips up an armchair—is decently handled, effectively expanding the action as written in the script for the better.

In the next, however, The Wolfman attempts to attack Costello while they're locked together in a hotel room. Typically, Costello goes off script. As a result, The Wolfman is so inept that he can't get the job done.

The third scene is the worst. Wildly expanding on the mild slapstick indicated in the screenplay, Costello repeatedly punches and kicks the hairy, inexplicably clumsy beast stalking him in the woods, believing it to be Abbott in a mask; this completely destroys any fear Chaney might generate.

And though his final scenes—which involve chasing Dracula—are handled more realistically,[7] the overall impression the film makes is that The Wolfman is a clown.

"Abbott and Costello ruined the horror films," Chaney will lament years later. "They made buffoons out of the monsters."

They certainly messed with Chaney's baby.

* * *

Tuesday, March 2, 1948. Barton is shooting at the concrete tank beyond the Phantom Stage. Chaney, Abbott, Costello, and Randolph are working. Meanwhile…

Rush hour.

Traffic is horribly backed up for blocks on the Hollywood Freeway. Police are about to arrest 17-year-old Ronald Chaney and his buddy Jack A. Arbuckle, 21.

The charge? Assault with a deadly weapon.

It all begins with a beer-fueled joyride.

Ron is driving. The friends amuse themselves by crowding other vehicles on the Cahuenga Pass, 745 feet up in the Santa Monica Mountains. The other drivers aren't happy about this, including Ernest S. Molnar, a 27-year-old art student.

Soon, Ron and Arbuckle start flinging beer bottles at adjacent cars. One such missile ends up smashing a windshield.[8]

Molnar has witnessed all of this. Unfortunately for him, Ron crowds his car next. Understandably agitated, Molnar forces Ron to pull over and confronts him.

Ron responds by repeatedly punching Molnar in the face while Arbuckle comes at him with a screwdriver. They cut up Molnar's eye pretty badly and smash his nose.

The cops show up and get Molnar to Hollywood Receiving hospital. Then, they call for a wagon to transport Ron and Arbuckle to the Hollywood police division.

But the call is misinterpreted as a cry for help, and suddenly every motorcycle cop under the sun is responding. Rubberneckers make a bad situation worse. Several hundred drivers are gridlocked.

Ron and Arbuckle aren't injured at all. They deny any wrongdoing. When questioned at the station, Ron gives his address as 12750 Hortense Street, North Hollywood—Chaney's house.

Arbuckle ends up in jail. Ron is sent to juvenile hall.

On Wednesday, March 3, *The Los Angeles Times* reports that Ron is Chaney's son. Chaney is back at work—they're shooting at the concrete tank again—but he can't be happy. This is a personal crisis. And no actor—or family—needs this kind of publicity.

Chaney and Patsy's reaction to Ron's behavior—as well as Dorothy's—is characteristically kept private. But it doesn't take a genius to guess that things can't be good over at the homestead.

Sadly, this isn't the last time Ron will be arrested.

When his father attempts suicide less than two months later, Ron tells the cops it was triggered by a "family argument." Can Ron's continued misbehavior—and perhaps his very presence in their house—be the source of tension between Chaney and Patsy?

No one has ever been able to confirm it. As we've seen, Patsy, Chaney's agent, and his attorney have all attempted to walk Ron's comments back. Under the circumstances, this is understandable.

But there is no denying that on the night of April 22, 1948, Lon Chaney Jr. decided that life was no longer worth living.

* * *

Monday, March 22, 1948. Chaney endures an almost 12-hour shoot wherein Talbot transforms in the woods. When Lon leaves at 7:50 PM, he's done with the film.

Friday, March 26. Production wraps up on what will be released as *Bud Abbott Lou Costello Meet Frankenstein*.[9] The movie will rake in $3.2 million, which is close to $350 million at this writing—a sizable hit.

Chaney gets third billing as "Lon Chaney."

Publicly, according to *The Oakland Tribune*, Chaney has made peace with the dropping of "Jr." by now:

"Sons and daughters of filmdom's great have made a name of their own—and all but a few have now dropped the 'Jr.' after their names. The latest to do this is the son of Lon Chaney. From now on he will be known as plain Lon Chaney. The son of one of the screen's all-time great artists, Lon's late father died in 1930."

Privately—though he's no longer known as Creighton—he'll never fully embrace the idea.

"I am most proud of the name Lon Chaney, because it was my father's, and he was something to be proud of," he'll say in 1969. "I am *not* so proud of Lon Chaney, Jr. because they had to starve me to make me take this name. Any ability that I might have had is *there*. The name didn't change it, but it certainly changed the income. So, *Junior* is a thing like a stick on my shoulder that I'd like to knock off, and I'd be happier without."

* * *

The very day production wraps on the Abbott and Costello film, columnist Edwin Schallert drops Chaney's name. It seems that producer Marcella Cisney is looking to revive *Of Mice and Me*n in Carmel as part of a tribute to author John Steinbeck. Cisney is looking to team Chaney up with Dane Clark as George.

On May 31, *Oakland Tribune* columnist Wood Soanes announces that, "So far as J. Arthur Rank is concerned, horror films are out...As a matter of fact, Hollywood came to that conclusion sometime back, and about the only horror films to be shown in recent days have been reissues. Boris Karloff, Bela Lugosi, Peter Lorre and Lon Chaney have turned to other fields of endeavor."

On June, 13—less than two months after Chaney's suicide attempt—John L. Scott of *The Los Angeles Times* announces that Chaney has been tentatively scheduled to revive *Of Mice and Men* with Gloria DeHaven and Mickey Knox. The play, produced by Brackett and Rathbun, is also slated for a week's run at the Lobero Theater in Santa Barbara beginning on July 14.

"This is the role which brought Lon his first recognition in the movie version of the sordid drama," explains *The Santa Maria Times*.

The revival gets good reviews:

"Having seen the original production of *Of Mice and Men* at the Music Box theatre in New York, with Broderick Crawford and Betty Field several years ago, we were in a position to compare the two performances," notes *The Lompoc Record*. "The Lobero presentation was excellent—it stacked up favorably with our earlier, estimable recollections of this play. Lon Chaney, son of the late screen make-up wizard, was outstanding in the role of the half-witted Lennie, good hearted hulk of a man who did not have enough sense to know the effects of his brute strength."

He may still bring the goods as Lennie. He may still remind folks of his screen triumph, not even ten years in the past. But this Lon Chaney is a different man than the 32-year-old version who got the break of a lifetime and knocked it out of the park.

That version had hope that the dream could come true.

This version knows that it's never going to happen.

Epilogue

Lon Chaney Jr. worked constantly during the 25 years of life that remained to him. There were moments of triumph—powerful bits in Stanley Kramer productions like *High Noon, Not as a Stranger*, and *The Defiant Ones*. There were bad films he was good in, such as *The Indestructible Man* and *The Black Sleep*. There were any number of parts in Westerns, parts that weren't much different from those he was assigned during his early days at RKO. And once in a while, there were roles in films that have since developed a cult following, like *Spider Baby*.

He even played a version of The Wolf Man twice more—in a comic episode on TV's *Route 66*, and in a horrible Mexican film called *Face of the Screaming Werewolf*.[1]

Life at home for him became easier when his sons were grown and gone,[2] though he doted on his grandchildren. He hunted and fished while physically able, and enjoyed watching sports and news on TV...but never his old films.

Part of the reason was his resentment of Universal. When he moved to the upper San Fernando Valley in the mid-1950s, he made his feelings clear:

"All my life I've wanted to look down on Universal Studios, and now at last I can."

Still, in 1957, he sold the rights to Lon senior's story to the studio so they could make *Man of a*

Thousand Faces, a biography starring James Cagney. As it turned out, he wasn't happy with the result.³

"You really whitewashed the son of a bitch, didn't you?" he said to screenwriter Robert Campbell.

He could never get past what his father had done, as an actor or a man.

* * *

As everyone who cares knows, Creighton Chaney had a dream: to make it in pictures on his own merits, and to top his father as an actor. Of course, he wasn't able to achieve either.

Yet he was wildly successful in his own right. He wasn't a major star like Clark Gable or Humphrey Bogart, but at the peak of his Universal days, he was making $3500 a week—worth about $2.4 million per year today. It's not nearly what top-grossing performers get now, but that kind of money is certainly more than most people will ever see.

Even after Universal dropped him, Chaney did reasonably well as a freelancer, financially if not always artistically. Sure, he felt like he had to work constantly, but his standard of living remained good. He never needed to tap into those hoarded canned goods.

And yet Chaney was unhappy.

Creighton Chaney wanted to be his father's son. But he was very much his mother's baby. Her genetics are stamped all over him: tall, good looking, talented. So are her personality traits: a sensitive nature, insecurity, depression. And unfortunately, so are her behaviors: extramarital affairs, a destructive taste for booze, an attempted suicide.

We know Creighton's father hated his mother. And by extension, he hated the parts of her that he could see in their son. This made his father fear for him. Lon tried to tough-love those traits out of him. He hurt Creighton deeply in the process, making the boy doubt himself.

There are gossipy Curt Siodmak stories about Lon beating Creighton with a strap, punishing the child for evils that had never taken place. Those in the know—Lon Ralph among them—say there is no truth to these yarns whatsoever.

But it might have been better if they were true.

At least then, Creighton might have forged a stronger defense against what he perceived to be Pop's disinterest. Physical abuse can lead to a victim to make a psychological break from an abuser, and ideally, a practical one as well—"I've gotta get out of here as soon as I can." But in Creighton's case, Lon's psychological tough-love method exacerbated rather than purged his issues.

Was Lon Chaney an abusive parent? Certainly not by the standards of his day, and probably not by the standards of today. Sure, Creighton was passed around from friends to relatives and didn't have a stable home until he was nine. But that's the story of a lot of folks, even now. Later, Creighton had ample food and creature comforts, and his father certainly taught him a work ethic.

Where Lon Chaney made his biggest error was in telling Creighton the lie that his mother was dead. It was unforgivable then, and it is unforgivable now. That Creighton found out only after Lon's death is tragic—he was never able to confront his father, and all of his previously good memories of Pop were tainted. His fight to obtain money from his father's estate—and his later attempts to top him in movies—were rooted, I believe, in resentment...a resentment he didn't want but couldn't shake.[4]

And Cleva? She might not have actually been dead, but in not fighting Lon harder in order to see her child, she might just as well have been.

Professionally, it ate at Creighton that he couldn't make it under his own name. It ate at him that he felt he had to bow his head and change it. It ate at him that Universal cast him in roles created by every other horror actor under the Hollywood sun...except for those of his father. He earned the equivalent of $2.4 million a year today, but he never got what he really wanted.

And so, he drank. He drank to have fun. He drank to forget. He drank just to drink—exactly like his mother. Patsy, who truly loved him, enabled him. It still wasn't enough.

Could he have lived his dream and topped his father? Almost certainly not. Lon Chaney was a major star who happened to make some horror films. He was in no way typecast. His only sound film, 1930's *The Unholy Three*, shows that he would have made the transition to talkies very well. Sure, his gestures and facial expressions in some scenes are cartoonish—whose weren't then?—and yeah, his highly-touted Old Lady voice is sometimes effective, sometimes not. He could not have pulled off Lennie—though he might have been great as George—and any Wolf Man he would have done would have been very different. Still, had he lived, Chaney would have been a force in the movies for years to come.

His son enjoyed about six years as a popular draw—for a then second-tier studio—and was typecast all the way. He would have done well as Quasimodo, but it's difficult to see him as The Phantom. Yet, he did better than the vast majority of film-actor wannabees, both before him and since.

What if *Of Mice and Men* had been a financial success and Chaney had starred in *Cup of Gold* for Hal Roach? Would he have then moved on to Laird Cregar-type roles—heavies, but heavies in A-productions at one of the Big Five? True, Cregar demonstrates a ferocity in *The Lodger* that Chaney probably couldn't have pulled off as well. But Chaney would have made a fine George Bone in *Hangover Square*.

What if some executive at Warner Brothers had seen Chaney as Larry Talbot confront gossiping villagers at Conliffe's shop in *The Wolf Man*, and thought, "He'd make a good Phillip Marlowe"? He would have—he matched Raymond Chandler's description of the character far better than did Bogie, and a tough, shrewd, wise-cracking American private detective would have been right in Chaney's wheelhouse.

Or what if Martin Howe in *High Noon* wasn't a bit? What if somebody thought a character study about Howe might make for a good picture?

What if...? What if...

Don G. Smith, Chaney Jr.'s biographer, asserts that Lon essentially gave up after attempting suicide in 1948.

"A Lon Chaney whose dreams had died left that hospital in 1948," he writes. "He was a different man, less self-assuming. Because of his fears, he had sometimes acted in the past as though he really hadn't cared, but that was an act, perhaps one of his best performances ever. Now pain had really taught him to no longer care, at least not as he had before."

I concur.

Director Reginald LeBorg believed Chaney chose a different way to kill himself after 1948: alcohol and sedatives.

"I made *The Mummy's Ghost* in the forties, and *The Black Sleep* was made about thirteen years later," LeBorg said. "But in his body, there was about twenty-five years' difference. With Chaney, I could see he was dying because his voice was different and his face was bloated, and he was drinking quite a bit. He knew he was going, and he didn't care anymore."

I concur.

This is not to say that Chaney's every waking moment was torture. Depression comes in waves, and he was certainly capable of enjoying life after 1948. His grandson Ron remembers him as fun-loving prankster. Chaney always did like kids.

But as he got older, he fell victim to a series of maladies that would cripple Job. Cataracts. Hepatitis. Gout. Beriberi. And throat cancer—doctors removed half of his vocal cords. None of these were helped by his constant drinking and smoking.

Yet he made news for preparing a comeback—a new stage version of *Of Mice and Men* wherein he was to use special throat mics.

But in more painful, private moments, colleagues heard him wish for death.

That wish came true on July 12, 1973. The 67-year-old actor suffered a heart attack and was pronounced dead late in the afternoon at his San Clemente home. As he wished, his body was donated to the USC School of Medicine.

* * *

Creighton Tull Chaney/Lon Chaney Jr. was a complicated man. He was bighearted, generous, intelligent, funny, and friendly. He was angry, prone to being petty, often drunk, occasionally mean, and sometimes violent. LeBorg once dubbed him "The Man of a Thousand Contradictions." The body of his work testifies to that as well: he was a generally good actor, capable of great-ness...but also capable of utter failure. Still, he created not one, but two signature characters: Lennie, and his baby The Wolf Man.[5] There are a lot of undiscovered acting talents who would give their right arms for that.

When I think of Chaney, I'm reminded of a passage by Walt Whitman:

> "Do I contradict myself?
> Very well then I contradict myself,
> (I am large, I contain multitudes.)"

I wonder if Chaney would ever have believed that the memory of him would last so long?

Acknowledgements

I first saw Lon Chaney, Jr. in *Abbott and Costello Meet Frankenstein*. WPIX, a regional station out of New York City, used to show A&C films on Sunday mornings, and—like a lot of late Baby-boom kids—I was hooked.

The Wolfman was my favorite. Since I hadn't seen any other Wolf Man films, I didn't realize at the time how much of a clown he was for A&C. But I found myself empathizing with the plight of Lawrence Talbot. I even asked some of my fourth-grade friends to start calling me "Talbert"—Bud Abbott's Jersey-accented version of the name.

Though my dad made his living as a correction officer, he was a gifted guitarist, singer, and photographer. My mom was an effective, compassionate elementary school teacher. Both of my parents were readers, and they encouraged my brother and me to read as well.

My dad had a book called *Karloff and Company: The Horror Film* by Robert F. Moss. I read and re-read that one, even though it was obvious Moss didn't care for Chaney, Jr. Moss even left *Frankenstein Meets the Wolf Man* out of his book entirely—I didn't know that film existed until months later, when TV accidentally ran it instead of the Mummy movie I was expecting.

Luckily, my friend John across the street had *Classics of the Horror Film* by William K. Everson. He wouldn't part with it no matter what I offered to trade him, but he did let me read from it just about every time I asked. I found Everson to be much more thorough than Moss.

I didn't read much of what I was assigned at school[1]—except, oddly, *Of Mice and Men*, which I loved and read straight through—but my nose was constantly buried in a book: *The Making of King Kong* by George Turner and Orville Goldner, *Heroes of the Horrors* by Calvin Thomas Beck, *The Horror People* by John Brosnan, and *Famous Monsters* magazine. I was always happy to drop everything and make a trip to the bookstore. Back then, you never knew what you were going to find. I still have dreams wherein I discover some previously unknown gem tucked away on a shelf stuffed with new hard-covers.

In those pre-video days, my dad would come shake us awake if he thought there was something late at night we needed to see. That's how, at 8, I saw *Bride of Frankenstein* for the first time.[2] Later, we scoured each issue of *TV Guide*, hoping that some cherished classic we hadn't yet seen would appear in the listings. When they were scheduled, it was usually deep in the night—what we'd later call, "Ass-o'clock." We'd set our alarms to get up and watch. That's how, at 13, I was introduced to *The Wolf Man*. I finally saw *Of Mice and Men* on WOR—also out of New York City—during my senior year in high school, and was very impressed. By then, I was known to my classmates as a skinny movie buff, amateur filmmaker, and trombone player who was always getting in trouble trying to be funny. But I'd seen *Citizen Kane*, *Treasure of the Sierra Madre*, *The Searchers*, and *Psycho* as well.

Of course, we collected as many of the Castle Films Super-8 digest versions of our favorites as we could, and later, the Universal-8 ones as well. We were the first family on our block to get a Betamax. And naturally, the first overpriced videos[3] we bought were of the horror classics.

Those writings, those Super-8 movies, and those clunky early videos have had a major impact on this book. So has the excellent work done more recently by Gregory William Mank and Suzanne Gargiulo. Plus, Don G. Smith's exhaustively researched *Lon Chaney, Jr.: Horror Film Star* is still the best comprehensive biography available, even though (at this writing), it's more than twenty years old.

Of all the classic horror stars—Leonidas "Lon" Chaney, Bela Lugosi, Boris Karloff, Lionel Atwill, and later, Vincent Price—I've always felt that Chaney Jr. was the most disrespected. He was harshly criticized for lacking charisma, which was often true, and for being ineffective, which was true only when he was miscast.[4] But much in the same way that being 'edgy' shouldn't be the sole way to define good rock music, chewing the scenery shouldn't define what makes good acting. Chaney *was* capable of chewing the scenery, and effectively—note the last few minutes in *The Wolf Man*. But evoking empathy—as both Chaney's father and Karloff had mastered—builds a rapport with audiences as well. And Chaney's best performances are textbook examples of that.

"Chaney Jr. always looked sincere, sometimes heartbreakingly so," historian Bernard F. Dick wrote in 1997, "especially when he was Larry Talbot in *The Wolf*

Man, undergoing the agony of metamorphosis…The truth is that Universal's horror cycle formerly ended with *The Wolf Man*; what followed was a 1940s freak show."

The way Chaney walked was thorny—sometimes through fault of his own, sometimes not. But like Larry Talbot before him, I hope he has found peace.

* * *

This book is a labor of love. No one commissioned it, and no one attempted to influence my thesis. I hope you've enjoyed it. I hope if Chaney's relatives ever read it, they sense that it comes from a good place: my desire to explore why one of the more talented people who has ever lived—and whom I've always admired—wanted to die…and at such a young age. I'm hoping that my insights on Chaney might help others to understand the emotional pain of those around them.

It's funny now, but the first full-length book I attempted to write—at age 13—was a production history of *The Wolf Man*. I didn't get very far, because research was a lot tougher back in those 'analog' days…and did I mention I was 13?

Oddly, until I actually started this project, I wasn't planning a book on Chaney at all. Rather, I was finishing the outline for the second volume of my Jeff Bridges biography when, on a whim, I decided to look into Chaney's suicide—you might recall from the **April**

22, 1948 chapter that I'd seen it treated more as a footnote in his life than the deadly serious event I hope to have proven here that it was.[5]

Of course, research can be a chain, and before long, I had piles of sources regarding the people and tragic events in Chaney's life, particularly in the months leading up to his suicide attempt. I'd never seen much of it in writing before.

I *had* to write this book.

First, my thanks go to Lon Chaney, Jr. I've seen most of his films, and—of course—have run some of them over and over again. The sympathy he was able to generate for his characters is still impressive. His work has provided me with hours of enjoyment. Yeah, he was flawed—who isn't?—but he also did a great deal of good, both on screen and in life. I only wish he had been happier in both.

Then, thanks go to my wife—artist, cake artist, and food artist Kim M. Simons—for not only designing the knock-out book cover but for understanding those times that I pretend to be watching TV with her while actually doing research. Being an extremely creative person herself, she understands the need I have to throw myself into my projects...and understands that, sometimes, I get lost. I love her unreservedly; we make a great team.

I'm grateful to my mom, too. She's always had a wicked sense of humor, but, moreover, she's always been supportive of my artistic endeavors...except for the time 15-year-old me and my 'tween-old brother attempted to make a splatter film in the back yard!

My brother is also a huge fan of classic horror films; he may know more about the Hammer films with Christopher Lee and Peter Cushing than anyone alive (what about a book of your own, Steve?). Then too, my grown sons—Mike and James—have always been interested in what I've been up to, whether it's writing, composing, or goin' solo with my rock band, The Misfit Toys.

Finally, I need to thank my father. He's gone a bit more than two years as I write, but he's alive in my thoughts and conversations every day. He was bright, wise, paranoid, stubborn, creative, funny, and totally devoted to my mom. He loved these films, he loved Lon Chaney, Jr., and he passed this love on to my brother and me. Like Chaney, my father was an alcoholic; unlike Chaney, my dad kicked the habit at age 48, and stayed sober for the rest of his 89 years.[6] I'm sorry he didn't get to see this book, because he would have been delighted by it.

Notes

April 22, 1948

[1] Salkow's brothers—Irving and Sidney—serve in the Marines.
[2] Woodmansee withdraws from the case before a jury concludes Chaplin is the father, despite blood tests proving the opposite; see Pirina, Garin. "How Charlie Chaplin Changed Paternity Laws in America." Mentalfloss.com, April 16, 2015. Web.
[3] It isn't even alluded to in a 1995 A&E *Biography* dedicated to Chaney featuring interviews with Chaney's grandson, though Chaney's depression and alcoholism are examined.

April 30, 1913

[1] Another brother named Earl dies in infancy in 1887.
[2] Much of my account of Cleva and Lon's marriage is drawn from *Lon Chaney's Shadow*, an excellent book written by Suzanne Gargiulo and published in 2009. I would highly recommend this book to Chaney fans of all stripes.
[3] For example, they will push the date of the wedding back to May 31, 1905, or they will push Creighton's birth ahead to February 10, 1907. At one point, Cleva even claims she and Lon were married three days after they met. Suzanne Gargiulo has done the definitive research on these matters.

[4] Years after Lon's death, Creighton begins telling the story that he was born dead and his father had to dip him in a freezing lake to revive him. As we will see, this story is fiction.

[5] "Baby" is a curious description—Creighton would have been seven.

January 5, 1935

[1] Chaney biographer Michael F. Blake describes Hastings as "legless." Chaney and Hazel knew each other—Chaney was, of course, still married to Cleva—and Hazel would babysit Creighton, saying she "grew fond of him" during this time.

[2] Years later, Curt Siodmak—screenwriter on *The Wolf Man*—will claim that Lon Jr. complained that his father often beat him physically. Lon Jr.'s son, Lon Ralph, told Chaney Sr. biographer Michael F. Blake that these accusations against his grandfather were "complete fiction." Lon Ralph believed his father may have told such tales to gain "sympathy and attention." Both Lon Jr. and Siodmak were known to have stretched the truth. (Blake, Michael F. *A Thousand Faces*.)

[3] This lesson will not be lost on Creighton. Later in life, he himself will hoard food (Senn, Bryan. "Man Made Monster." *Lon Chaney Jr.* Baltimore: Midnight Marquee Press, 1997, p. 31. Print).

[4] Creighton's actual height is hard to pin down. Late in life, he mentioned the 6-inch shoes he wore in *Of Mice and Men* (1939), causing Calvin Thomas Beck to write, "In reality he was just six feet tall." "From that film on,"

Chaney is quoted, "people thought I was much taller" (see Beck, p. 235).

Then, Creighton's father claimed his own height to be 5'9" in 1924 (*Photoplay*)—an exaggeration of two inches. Perhaps he exaggerated his son's height as well?

Also, Philip Riley quotes a Universal press release from *The Wolf Man* (1941), stating, "Chaney came off second best in a fight with Claude Rains, although he out-measured his opponent by 60 pounds and five inches…Rains accidentally clubbed Chaney in the right eye with the silver head of a cane, which weighs ten pounds." Rains claimed a height of 5'7" (see Riley, p. 60).

Creighton himself often claimed a height of 6'3"—as his duplicate driver's license issued on June 22, 1942—and pictured on the internet—attests:

(https://www.pinterest.at/pin/341218109239112544/

However, actor Mikey Knox—who played George to Chaney's Lennie in a 1948 stage revival of *Mice* in Santa Barbara—had an issue with this: "In one of the stories somebody wrote about the play, they interviewed him and he said he was 6'3". I don't think he was because he wore extra-high heels in his shoes to get the height. If he had been 6'3" and added another three inches with heels, I'd have noticed. It didn't seem to me he was *that* tall" (see Weaver, Chapter 8).

Finally, when comparing Chaney in films with other actors—particularly a face-to-face profile confrontation with Patrick Knowles (who claimed to be 6'2") in *Frankenstein Meets the Wolf Man* (1943)—it's pretty safe to say that Creighton was in actuality closer to 72-73 inches tall than 75.

[5] Gargiulo identifies him as W.W. Greenwood.

August 28, 1930

[1] There are conflicting reports as to exactly when Creighton discovered that his father and stepmother were deceiving him. Reliable sources indicate that it was either just before the premier of *The Phantom of the Opera* in 1925, or shortly after his father's death in 1930. Given the investigation initiated by Adela Rogers St. Johns in 1930, I'm inclined to go with the latter. Readers are encouraged to decide for themselves.

[2] According to actor James Cagney, who plays Chaney Sr. in *Man of a Thousand Faces* (1957)—and who co-stars with Lon Jr. in *A Lion Is in the Streets* (1953)—the reunion between Creighton and Cleva was painful. Allegedly, Chaney knocks on Cleva's door and a lady answers. When Creighton asks about Cleva Chaney, he's told she doesn't live there. And then a man calls out from inside: "Who is it, Cleva?" (Cagney, James. *Cagney By Cagney*).

February 10, 1932

[1] Creighton believes himself to be 25. As we've seen, his father and mother misrepresented his actual birthdate so as to cover up their unwed status at the time he was born. According to Suzanne Gargiulo, this will eventually cost Creighton some Social Security benefits (Gargiulo, Endnotes).
[2] The casting doesn't materialize.
[3] Actually released as *The Sport Parade*.
[4] "The first morning I was to make a fifteen-foot leap from a tree to the back of a moving horse," he'll tell Wood Soanes in 1933. He also claims to have "smashed a couple of bones" in another leap, and to have suffered "a broken hand, torn shoulder ligaments, and a beautiful black eye" in an on-screen fight with actor Joe Bonomo (Soanes, p. 33).
[5] Interestingly, *The San Francisco Examiner* runs this brief in December: "Believe it or not, Creighton Chaney does not enjoy kissing a girl. He admitted to some of his friends that he doesn't care for leading man roles because the studio always insists that he kiss the leading lady…Radio Pictures has done its best to make a leading man of him. They might succeed if he didn't have this aversion to making love to the leading ladies" (December 4, 1932, p. 37. Print). Is Chaney here trying to mollify Dorothy, who probably suspects that he's having affairs?

October 31, 1933

[1] Obituaries will report that she is 43 at the time of her death, but this is incorrect.

[2] On June 25, Creighton will come across columnist Robert Grandon. "Met Creighton Chaney on the street," Grandon will write on June 26, "tall and bronzed as an Indian…full of enthusiasm and anecdotes regarding his mining claim. 'I've got a ranch down at Sutter's Mill, Bob,' he told me. 'It's right on the site of the original gold discovery in '49…and, boy, maybe thar's gold in them thar hills yet…who can say?'" (Grandon, Robert. "Telling on Hollywood." *Courier-Journal.* June 26, 1933, p. 12. Print). As it turns out, there wasn't any more gold there.

[3] The very same hospital where her husband died.

[4] "The stepson was kept away from Hazel's hospital room, yet her sister Eleanor, brother Charles, and Jeske visited her bedside every day to cheer her up and take care of any business. It wasn't Hazel's illness that kept Creighton away. He must have known that" (Gargiulo, *Lon Chaney's Shadow*).

[5] "Mrs. Chaney desired a death-bed marriage with her chauffeur in order to prevent unfriendly relatives of her late husband…from obtaining any of her wealth" ("Reveal Motives Behind Intended Chaney Marriage." *Edwardsville Intelligencer.* Nov. 2, 1933). These unfriendly relatives certainly included Creighton Chaney.

June 25, 1936

[1] According to Suzanne Gargiulo, "it's easy to believe Joy Parker and Creighton Chaney knew each other well and spoke of their pain and humiliation" (Gargiulo, *Lon Chaney's Shadow*). She stops short, however, of implicating Chaney in the kidnapping plot.

[2] It's likely that Chaney and Davey are more than just friends—as Suzanne Gargiulo notes, Chaney is seeing a lot of women on the side at this juncture and will be divorced before the year is out. But since a romantic relationship between them can't be conformed without any doubt, the reader is free to assume that I'm speculating.

[3] Certainly an interesting business for Chaney—with his growing drinking problem—to be in.

[4] To be fair, he's billed in the film as Creighton Chaney.

[5] According to Don G. Smith, "Drake tried to scotch the idea. This angered Chaney and initiated a short period of estrangement between the two men" (Smith, p. 21).

[6] *The Fresno Bee*, Jan. 11, 1938, p. 16.

[7] "Patsy tried to comfort Creighton as best as she could, even when he was drunk and violent. She understood his moods and was willing to do whatever it took to stay with him. In between the bouts of drunken rage he was a very kind person with a good heart and fun to be with. Creighton too often let his demons get the best of him and his depression became intolerable. He had to drink to stay sane, but this kind of sanity was only an illusion and a way to avoid dealing with the darker side of his nature" (Gargiulo, *Lon Chaney's Shadow*).

[8] "According to Elena Verdugo [Chaney's co-star in *House of Frankenstein*], a story once circulated at Universal that Lon sometimes physically abused his wife Patsy. 'As the story goes,' Verdugo said, 'Patsy secretly took karate lessons. The next time Lon hit her, Patsy knocked him on his butt. After that, he never laid a hand on her again. Of course, the story might not have been true'" (Smith, p. 97).

[9] According to Don G. Smith, "My impression is that Patsy developed all the coping strategies common to wives of alcoholics. She was, in essence, his caretaker and possibly a surrogate mother. All research on the subject indicates that families containing alcoholics are not well-adjusted, happy units. The Chaneys were probably no exception" (Smith, p. 189).

[10] "According to [actor] Robert Quarry, Lon definitely had a proclivity for violence against women. 'When we were both at Universal,' Quarry said, 'Lon was having an affair with a young woman who booked films into the screening room. Sometimes after being with him, she would come to work wearing dark glasses to hide black eyes, or she would have bruises. One day I asked her, "Why do you put up with it?" She said, "He's very sweet when he's sober." Of course, that wasn't very often'" (Smith, p. 97).

[11] Behind *Gone with the Wind* and *Mr. Smith Goes to Washington*.

[12] A bit more than $67,000 as of this writing—and an interesting figure, given that if he'd earned any more, he'd legally have to cough up 20% of the overage to Dorothy.

October 27, 1941

[1] Some of Chaney's statements here need to be taken with a grain of salt. To begin with, his father had extensive experience on stage, so he certainly could memorize long speeches. Then, too, his father—at five-seven—was of average height, not "a little guy."

[2] According to Don G. Smith, the studio also considered Orson Welles! This would have been a terrible idea (Smith, p. 24).

[3] This story sounds a little contrived, but it could be true.

[4] *Citizen Kane* will premiere at El Capitan in 1941.

[5] *Of Mice and Men* will be her film debut.

[6] Among Chaney's detractors, there has been a tendency to denigrate even this almost unanimously praised performance. The authors of *Universal Horrors*, for example, have this to say: "Lennie almost couldn't be played badly and was an ideal showcase for any young actor" (Brunas, Brunas, Weaver, p. 244). This is patently untrue; even Chaney's father wouldn't have been good as Lennie. Moreover, Brod Crawford says in 1981, "He made it completely different from mine, and it was a damn fine role" (*Filmfax*, p. 56).

[7] Patsy also claims to have been offered the part of Mae's understudy for El Capitan's stage production, but turns it down. "I didn't want to act, he [Chaney] discouraged me" (*Filmfax*, p. 53).

[8] Beck, p. 235.

[9] Frank S. Nugent at *The New York Times* does opine that Chaney's performance doesn't quite erase the memory of Brod Crawford's on Broadway.

[10] The novel details the exploits of Captain Henry Morgan, pirate and privateer. Though Morgan had been the inspiration for Errol Flynn's *Captain Blood* back in 1935, as of 1939, no one in Hollywood had yet played Morgan himself. It's interesting to speculate how Chaney's career might have been different had the film been made. When Roach scotches plans for *Cup of Gold*, it falls to Laird Cregar to play Morgan for the first time in 1942's *The Black Swan*…which Cregar does with great flair.

[11] Griffith and Roach battle over story, tone, and special effects. Griffith wants 3D animation, *a la* KING KONG (1933); Roach shoots live lizards instead and blows them up on screen via process shots. Griffith takes his name off the film. Ironically, *One Million B.C.* is nominated for the Best Special Effects Oscar.

[12] Atwill is an odd character in real life as well, noted for attending murder trials and being chauffeured around in an automobile riddled with bullet holes (Anger, p. 94). The nadir of his notoriety will commence just after this film is finished shooting: he'll host a Christmastime orgy at his home which will come back to haunt him in 1942 (Mank, p. 98).

[13] Dan McCormick is a role well suited to Chaney's strengths—an average Joe in abnormal circumstances who is to be pitied as much as feared. Universal doesn't always understand this, however, and often miscasts him to the detriment of his reputation.

[14] These are MGM, RKO, 20th Century Fox, Paramount, and Warner Brothers.

[15] Try it: "Place 6 slices of drained pineapple in a flat baking dish. Add 1 cup of Mogen David Wine, 3

tablespoons cooking fat and ¼ cup minced parsley, and juice of one lemon over pineapple. Bake for 10 minutes, then place over chops and broil together in moderate to hot oven. Mint jelly may be used if desired…1 tablespoon for each slice of pineapple."

[16] In actuality, the film was nominated, not Chaney.

[17] What follows is in no way a complete history of the production of *The Wolf Man*. Readers who desire to know the specific details are invited to seek out *The Wolf Man: The Original Shooting Script* (Philip Riley, ed. © 1993, MagicImages Productions), an excellent source from which I've drawn a great deal of my account.

[18] In actuality, the hands are gloves, and the feet are boots—the feet even make a Chaney-less appearance during the climax of Universal's *Night Monster* (1942).

[19] Dorst was 21 at the time.

[20] It's interesting that *The Wolf Man* features no scene wherein Talbot's face is shown transforming into the monster. Such scenes will be a staple in the sequels.

[21] According to Patsy Chaney, "He didn't like her. He called her 'Shankers.' Evelyn Shankers" (*Filmfax*, p. 53).

[22] Ironically, the bear is cut completely from the released film. According to Greg Mank, "[T]he studio probably cut the scene because the shots of Chaney beating and bellowing at the bear would have upset animal lovers and lost sympathy for Larry Talbot…Universal has yet to find the cut bear footage in the studio archives" (*The Wolf Man: The Original Shooting Script*, p. 63). It's also possible that the finished scene was chopped because it wasn't very good. In the one still that survives, it's obvious that it's not Chaney grappling with the bear.

²³ Interestingly, Lugosi had lobbied for the lead role in *The Wolf Man*. According to Siodmak, "[H]e was a pest. He always called me and said, 'Curt! Can you get me zat part? Huh? I want to play zat part!'…He could never act his way out of a paper bag!" (Mank, p. 113).

August 17, 1944

¹ Izaak "Ike" Walton was a noted outdoorsman and author (*The Compleat Angler*).
² Lon Ralph is 16; Ron is 14.
³ Burrell will open a men's clothing store in Sacramento, which he'll operate for more than 50 years. He dies in 2007, leaving behind a wife, a daughter, a son, two stepchildren, and two grandkids.
⁴ Boyer is the French-born star of *Algiers* (1938), and is noted for his charm.
⁵ Aside from a hairpiece, that is—interesting, in that Chaney himself never gets bald.
⁶ Which is very good….
⁷ Ironically, Lugosi had turned down the part in 1931, resulting in Karloff's big break. Also of interest (according to Greg Mank): "Surprisingly, Chaney recognized Frankenstein's creation as the top horror of Universal's repertoire, and he initially griped that he wanted the Monster role. A perusal of the script, in which the Wolf Man dominated, changed his mind, as did his affection for the lycanthropic Talbot" (Mank, p. 113).
⁸ His shirt collar is open, for example, necessitating more yak hair and shredded kelp glued to his neck and chest.

In addition, his clothes are lighter than their black counterparts in *The Wolf Man*.

[9] Chaney is known to have had occasional affairs; could this have been one of them? There is no "smoking gun" evidence, so readers are encouraged to judge for themselves.

[10] Chaney comes out okay, and even makes it a point to bring the horse a daily sugar treat. Ouspenskaya breaks her ankle and finishes the film with a hidden cast.

[11] Born Harry Ueberroth, Curtis was an American actor (*Buck Privates*). He and Massey were married from 1941-1942.

[12] The first close-up of The Monster in the film isn't even Lugosi—it's Perkins.

[13] Of course, film buffs would love to see the footage today, but Universal has yet to find it…if they're even looking.

[14] They married on September 6, 1942. Denning will serve on a submarine for three years.

[15] It's interesting to note how Chaney keeps getting taller.

[16] His shirt collar is open wider, his beard is thicker, and the hair on both his gloves and feet is longer. In addition, his clothes are darker than in *Frankenstein Meets The Wolf Man*, though his shirt features only one flapped pocket instead of two. A notable error is made when Talbot transforms while looking into a mirror—the reflection clearly shows that the actor is not wearing the hairy gloves. Interestingly, The Wolf Man's death scene features Chaney's own agonized gasps—the only time he hasn't been overdubbed with actual wolf sounds while in character.

[17] He also builds an airport at Lennie's Ranch.

[18] When he doesn't, they sue, claiming Chaney agreed to the payment. Chaney denies this.

[19] My son Mike always found this to be interesting. Talbot: "I'm in agony because I kill people every month. But I think I'd look good in a mustache." Chaney wore a mustache in many of his films during this period.

[20] He also has his black shirt back, though the button-down flap pockets are gone.

[21] As it turns out, Lon and Patsy are recording skits on records which they send to friends. The cop advises them to keep it down…and joins them for the session!—*San Fernando Valley Times*, March 26, 1945, p. 24.

[22] His brother Ron will also be six feet tall. They'll both work with their mother at the water heater company in the 1950s.

[23] "All of his personal effects were left in his hotel room," the cops report. They undertake a search. Lo and behold, Hallock is found alive and well at home in Denver. He instructs the hotel to send his things.

[24] Another informal club is called The American Society of Motion Picture Villains Inc. In addition to Chaney, members include Peter Lorre, Claude Rains, Sydney Greenstreet, Boris Karloff, Vincent Price, Alan Ladd, and founder/president George Macready.

[25] Symptoms include fevers, sweats, weakness, anorexia, headache, and muscle pain.

[26] Cleva Creighton's second husband.

February 5, 1948

[1] The ad, entitled "He Ruled a Raw Frontier," features a cartoon version of Chaney on the set of *Albuquerque* endorsing the product: "Trim Hair Tonic gives you the best looking hair by far!" It can be found in the archives of *The San Francisco Examiner*.

[2] According to Bob Thomas, Costello had resented Abbott since 1937 because he'd had to bribe Abbott with a bigger salary cut in order to convince him to play Atlantic City. As it turned out, the Atlantic City gigs really broke the act. In 1942—never one to forget a slight—Costello demanded a sixty-forty split in his favor, plus a change in billing to "Costello and Abbott." An enraged Abbott agreed to the split, but not the billing. Universal backed him, and Costello never forgave either of them.

[3] In the final draft, The Mummy and The Son of Dracula are axed, and The Invisible Man is reduced to a bit.

[4] "I think the only person Lugosi ever disliked was Lon Chaney Jr.," Don Marlowe, Lugosi's agent, said (Lenning, p. 363). Yet Lugosi is a heavy drinker himself, as Gregory William Mank explains in *It's Alive*: "Lugosi, whose professional ethics were far too high for him to even consider sipping his beloved brew of Scotch and beer during soundstage hours, consequently had strong feelings about his flask-brandishing co-star." Sadly, Lugosi is also addicted to narcotics, due to "a medical gaffe in 1944" (Mank). Regarding his resentment of Chaney's casting in Son of Dracula, Arthur Lennig in *The Immortal Count* states, "Lugosi was astounded to hear that Universal did not even

consider him for what had been for fifteen years his most noteworthy role, but instead chose the painfully miscast Chaney. He was not only hurt; he was enraged."

[5] Unfortunately for Chaney, the entire transformation will have to be reshot on March 13, resulting in a more than 12-hour day for him. ; LaVigne notes that he was a little wary of applying glue all over Chaney after the actor had been drinking.

[6] Unfortunately, Thurston catches some shards of fake glass in her eyes and has to go to the hospital. Universal ups her pay for the job to $300 (from $55).

[7] The scenes are partially handled by doubles: Walter DePalma for Chaney, Bud Wolfe for Lugosi.

[8] *The Valley Times* reports that Molnar's windshield is shattered, but *The Los Angeles Times* has Molnar stating that a "hurtling beer bottle" smashed against a "third man's windshield."

[9] This is actually the title as it appears onscreen. Of course, the film will come to be known as *Abbott and Costello Meet Frankenstein*—the title Universal announces on March 1.

Epilogue

[1] Technically, he's not Larry Talbot in either one. On TV, he plays himself; in the 1959 movie, he's a revived mummy who just happens to also be a werewolf!

[2] In June of 1949, Ron—by then a sailor in the U.S. Navy, stationed at Millington Naval Base—was arrested for stealing—and trying to pawn—a ceiling fan from a Memphis, TN hotel. He was held pending a $500 bond. "I was broke and didn't want to ask my mother for

money," Ron told the police. He also claimed to have never been in trouble before, which we know isn't true. Dorothy—by then heading up the water heater company, and remarried to Loren G. Symons—bailed him out. Ron eventually married and got into ranching. He died in 1987. His son, Ronald Curt Chaney, serves at this writing as the family spokesperson.

Chaney's mother, Cleva Creighton, was also arrested in 1949 on a drunk charge at a Pasadena beauty parlor. Cleva died of a stroke on November 21, 1967, at a Sierra Madre convalescent home. She was 78.

Lon Ralph worked with his mother at the corporation. He was married to Constance Griffith in 1948. Later in life, Lon Ralph spoke candidly to biographer Michael Blake about his father's attempts to win sympathy through exaggeration. He was known for being a slow-growth activist in Fallbrook, his adopted hometown. Sadly, Lon Ralph was killed in a one-truck accident on May 4, 1992. He was 64.

[3] Chaney would later say that he'd written a script for the film, but Universal hired a bunch of writers to change it. However, screenwriter Robert Campbell said Chaney had nothing to do with the writing—no draft, no story conferences, no nothing. A Chaney script has never materialized, though he was a good writer, as his existing letters attest. At the time of his death, he was writing a coffee table book called *A Century of Chaneys*, going back to his grandfather Frank. His grandson Ron has said that he's going to finish the project.

[4] Columnist Adela Rogers St. Johns, who knew both father and son, believed this to be true, as we've seen in the **August 28, 1930** chapter.
[5] Sadly, he watched them both become objects of ridicule—Lennie in a series of Warner Brothers' cartoons, and The Wolfman in *Abbott and Costello Meet Frankenstein*. The sale of Universal's horror films to TV in the late 1950s reinvigorated interest in his work, however, and Chaney was gratified.

Acknowledgements

[1] I read them all later and then some, since I ended up teaching high school English for 30 years.
[2] The part where they take the bandages off of the bride and she's staring back in close-up scared the hell out of me.
[3] I paid $69.99 for the 1976 remake of *King Kong* on Betamax—the equivalent of nearly $200 in mid-2021.
[4] Which was too often, particularly at Universal, where the suits were understandably more worried about making payroll than they were about Chaney's reputation.
[5] Don G. Smith's book is a notable exception.
[6] I think this is why much of Chaney's story resonates with me. Though my dad was ultimately a good man, my early years—particularly from the ages of 13 through 16—were often filled with deception, arguments, accidents, hospitalizations, and the like—all of which caused trust issues for me. Like Chaney, my dad told me he drank because he felt like my grandfather considered him to be inadequate. This father-son dynamic can be

powerful, as Creighton Chaney certainly knew. I admired my father's unshakable devotion to sobriety—he kicked a one-to-two-quart bottle-of-vodka-a-day habit—but I questioned everything I'd been taught and went down some rough roads. In my mid-30s, I came to grips with my complaints about my youth, and don't dwell on them anymore. Today, my view can best be described as, "In general, people do the best they can. If they let you down, it's more about them than about you. Just try to understand." I can also relate to Patsy and Lon's struggle with blended families, which can be emotionally devastating…as the vast majority of those who have been divorced and remarried with kids in the picture can attest.

Sources

April 22, 1948

Blake, Michael F. *A Thousand Faces*. Lanham/New York/Oxford: Vestal Press, 1995. Ebook.

Blake, Michael F. *Lon Chaney: The Man Behind the Thousand Faces*. Lanham, MD: The Vestal Press, 1990. Print.

"Bud Abbott Lou Costello Meet Frankenstein." *AFI Catalog*. Afi.com. Web.

"Chaney Gains on Ill Effect of Sleep Pills." *Valley Times* (North Hollywood, California). April 24, 1948, p. 2. Print.

"Chaney 'Just Fair'; Listed as Attempted Suicide Case." *News-Pilot*. April 23, 1948, p. 1. Print.

"Chaney Reported in Semicoma, but Improved." *Los Angeles Times, The* (Los Angeles, California). April 24, 1948, p. 19. Print.

Gourley, Jack and Gary Dorst. "A Man, A Myth, and Many Monsters." *Filmfax*. May 1990. Print.

"L.A. Girl Accuses Chaplin As Father of Unborn Child." *San Francisco Examiner, The* (San Francisco, California). June 4, 1943, pp. 1 and 13. Print.

"Lon Chaney Fights Against Pill Death." *Valley Times* (North Hollywood, California). April 23, 1948, pp. 1 and 2. Print.

"Lon Chaney Is Reported Improving." *Times Dispatch, The* (Richmond, VA). April 24, 1948, p. 7. Print.

"Lon Chaney Jr. Gains." *Boston Globe, The* (Boston, Massachusetts). April 26, 1948, p. 20. Print.

"Lon Chaney, Jr., Gravely Ill After Taking Sedatives." *Rock Island Argus, The* (Illinois). April 23, 1948, p. 1. Print.

"Lon Chaney, Jr., in Attempt at Suicide." *Daily Times, The* (Davenport, Iowa). April 23, 1948, p. 18. Print.

"Lon Chaney, Jr., In 'Serious Condition'." *Frederick Leader, The* (Frederick, Oklahoma). April 23, 1948, p. 1. Print.

"Lon Chaney, Jr., in Suicide Attempt." *Daily Standard, The* (Sikeston, Missouri). April 23, 1948, p. 1. Print.

"Lon Chaney Jr. Takes Too Many Sleeping Pills." *Los Angeles Times, The* (Los Angeles, California). April 23, 1948, p. 1. Print.

"Lon Chaney Jr. Tries to Kill Self." *Dayton Herald, The* (Dayton, Ohio). April 23, 1948, p. 11. Print.

"Lon Chaney, Jr. Weds." *Lincoln Star, The* (Lincoln, Nebraska). January 10, 1938, p. 1. Print.

"Lon Chaney Recovers from Drug Overdose." *Oakland Tribune* (Oakland, California). April 29, 1948, p. 21. Print.

"Lon Chaney Takes 40 Sleeping Pills After Family Spat." *Dispatch, The* (Molene, Illinois). April 23, 1948, p. 31. Print.

Mank, Gregory William. *It's Alive!* San Diego/New York: A.S. Barnes & Co., 1981. Print.

"Mrs. Chaney Divorces Son of Late Thespian." *Los Angeles Times, The* (Los Angeles, CA). July 25, 1936, p. 4. Print.

Svehla, Gary J. and Susan, eds. *Lon Chaney, Jr.* Baltimore: Midnight Marquee Press, 1997. Print.

Valley Times. Headlines. April 22, 1948. Print.

"War Finally Is Over for The Salkows." *Valley Times* (North Hollywood, California). March 16, 1946, p. 11. Print.

"Wife Denies Lon Chaney Attempted Suicide." *Sacramento Bee, The* (Sacramento, CA). April 24, 1948, p. 7. Print.

April 30, 1913

Blake, Michael F. *Lon Chaney, The Man Behind the Thousand Faces*. Lanham, MD: Vestal Press, 1990. Print.

Blake, Michael F. *Thousand Faces, A*. Lanham/New York/Oxford: Vestal Press, 1995. Ebook.

Gargiulo, Suzanne. *Lon Chaney's Shadow*. Bearmanor Media, 2009. Ebook.

"Stage Manager's Wife Tries to End Life.*"* *Los Angeles Evening Express* (Los Angeles, California). May 1, 1913, p. 13. Print.

St. Johns, Adela Rogers. "Lon Chaney's Love and Work Here." *Daily Oklahoman, The* (Oklahoma City, Oklahoma). May 17, 1931, p. 51. Print.

St. Johns, Adela Rogers. "Love, Laughter and Tears." *Cincinnati Enquirer, The (*Cincinnati, Ohio). December 3, 1950, p. 224. Print.

"Stage Manager's Wife Tries To End Life." *Los Angeles Evening Express* (Los Angeles, California). May 1, 1913, p. 13. Print.

January 5, 1935

"America's Miracle: Free Enterprise in Action in Southern California—General Water Heater Corp." *Los Angeles Times, The* (Los Angeles, CA). March 20, 1956, p. 14. Print.

Beck, Calvin Thomas. *Heroes of the Horrors*. New York: Collier Books, 1975. Print.

Blake, Michael F. *Lon Chaney, The Man Behind the Thousand Faces*. Lanham, MD: Vestal Press, 1990. Print.

Brosnan, John. *Horror People, The*. New York: Plume, 1976. Print.

Gargiulo, Suzanne. *Lon Chaney's Shadow*. Bearmanor Media, 2009. Ebook.

Gourley, Jack and Gary Dorst. "A Man, A Myth, and Many Monsters." *Filmfax*. May 1990. Print.

Hennessey, Eileen. "Society." *Los Angeles Evening Express* (Los Angeles, CA). November 15, 1926, p. 6. Print.

Keavey, Hubbard. "Screen Life in Hollywood." *Morning Union, The*. Feb. 27, 1932, p. 6. Print.

"Licensed to Wed." *Visalia Times-Delta*. April 1, 1919, p. 8. Print.

"Lon Chaney's Son Plans to Assume Name for Screen." *Indianapolis Star, The* (Indianapolis, Indiana). January 5, 1935, p. 11. Print.

Mank, Gregory William. *It's Alive!* San Diego/New York: A.S. Barnes & Co., 1981. Print.

Riley, Philip (ed.) *Wolf Man, The: The Original Shooting Script*. Abescon, NJ: MagicImage Filmbooks, 1993. Print.

St. Johns, Adela Rogers. "Love, Laughter and Tears." *Cincinnati Enquirer, The* (Cincinnati, Ohio). December 3, 1950, p. 224. Print.

Svehla, Gary J. and Susan, eds. *Lon Chaney, Jr.* Baltimore: Midnight Marquee Press, 1997. Print.

Thomas, Dan. "Chaney's Son, in Movies, Won't Copy Famous Dad. *Seminole Producer*. Feb. 28, 1932, p. 9. Print.

Weaver, Tom. *Sci-Fi Swarm and Horror Horde, A*. Jefferson, North Carolina: McFarland & Company, Inc., 2010. Ebook.

"You will ask for $150 a week from now on." *Miami Herald, The*. December 10, 1950, p. 31. Print.

August 28, 1930

Associated Press. "Lon Chaney Rite to Be Simple Tribute." *Colton Daily Courier*. Aug. 27, 1930, p. 1. Print.

Blake, Michael F. *A Thousand Faces*. Lanham/New York/Oxford: Vestal Press, 1995. Ebook.

Blake, Michael F. *Lon Chaney, The Man Behind the Thousand Faces*. Lanham, MD: Vestal Press, 1990. Print.

Brosnan, John. *Horror People, The*. New York: Plume, 1976. Print.

"Chaney Gives Dollar to His Divorced Wife." *Times-Tribune, The.* Sept. 5, 1930, p. 19. Print.

Fidler, Jimmie. "More money…" *Times, The.* Oct. 27, 1941, p. 5. Print.

"Frances C. Bush, Lon Chaney Widow." *Morning Call, The.* Nov. 23, 1967, p. 24. Print.

Gargiulo, Suzanne. *Lon Chaney's Shadow.* Bearmanor Media, 2009. Ebook.

Henderson, Sam. "Secrets from Lon Chaney's Oklahoma Odyssey. *Daily Oklahoman.* Nov. 14, 1982, p. 202. Print.

"I always got the impression that the boy never quite forgave his father…" *Miami Herald, The.* Dec. 10, 1950, p. 31. Print.

"Lon Chaney Is Seriously Ill at Hospital in L.A." *Sacramento Bee.* August 23, 1930, p. 1. Print.

Riley, Philip, ed. *The Wolf Man (The Original Shooting Script).* Absecon, NJ: MagicImage Filmbooks, 1993. Print.

San Francisco Examiner, The. Lon Chaney's Hand Camera Film. April 12, 1931, p. 86. Print.

St. Johns, Adela Rogers. "Lon Chaney's Love and Work Here." *Daily Oklahoman.* May 17, 1931, p. 51. Print.

St. Johns, Adela Rogers. "Love, Laughter and Tears." *Cincinnati Enquirer.* Dec. 3, 1950, p. 224. Print.

"Strange Wills." *Muscatine Journal.* March 1, 1978, p. 58. Print.

February 10, 1932

"America's Miracle: Free Enterprise in Action in Southern California." *Los Angeles Times, The*. March 20, 1956, p. 14. Print.

Beck, Calvin Thomas. *Heroes of the Horrors*. New York: Collier Books, 1975. Print.

Chaney Teaches McCrae to Wrestle. *Shreveport Journal, The*. Sept. 10, 1932, p. 4. Print.

"Chaneys, The." *Harrisburg Telegraph*. Nov. 7, 1932, p. 14. Print.

"Creighton Chaney Signs." *Los Angeles Times, The*. May 24, 1932, p. 7. Print.

Dowling, Mark and Lynn Norris. "Hollywood Speaking." *Arcadia Tribune*. March 25, 1932, p. 5. Print.

Gargiulo, Suzanne. *Lon Chaney's Shadow*. Bearmanor Media, 2009. Ebook.

He'll Woo Fame Under Own Name." *Los Angeles Times, The*. Feb. 3, 1932, p. 18. Print.

"Hollywood Report, The." *News-Democrat and Leader*. Jan. 3, 1935, p. 7. Print.

Keavey, Hubbard. "Screen Life in Hollywood." *Morning Union, The*. Feb. 27, 1932, p. 6. Print.

"Little Grandson of Chaney Hurt." *Los Angeles Times, The*. May 4, 1932, p. 28. Print.

"Lon Chaney's Son Balks at Using Father's Name." *Los Angeles Times, The*. Jan. 27, 1932, p. 19. Print.

"Looks, Not Name, Count." *Manhattan Mercury, The*. Feb. 16, 1932, p. 4. Print.

Parsons, Louella O. "Metro-Goldwyn-Mayer registered a violent protest." *Sacramento Bee, The*. Feb. 7, 1932, p. 20. Print.

Parsons, Louella O. "Sons, Daughters of Movie Stars Have Hard Road. *Honolulu Advertiser, The.* May 1, 1932, p. 34. Print.

Pryor, Nancy. "Is Lon Chaney's Son Fated to Suffer fir Films, Too?" *Movie Classic.* Jan. 1933, p. 54. Print.

Shippey, Lee. "The Lee Side o' L.A." *Los Angeles Times, The.* Feb. 7, 1932, p. 28. Print.

Smith, Don G. Lon Chaney, Jr.: *Horror Film Star.* Jefferson NC: McFarland and Company, 1996. Print.

"Son of Lon Chaney Plans Career as Actor in Films." *San Bernardino County Sun.* Jan. 27, 1932, p. 1. Print.

"Son of Lon Chaney Signed for Talkies." *Pittsburgh Press, The.* Feb. 18, 1932, p. 14. Print.

Thirer, Irene. "Chaney Jr. Gets Starring Role." *Daily News.* June 20, 1932, p. 242. Print.

Thomas, Dan. "Chaney's Son, in Movies, Won't Copy Famous Dad. *Seminole Producer.* Feb. 28, 1932, p. 9. Print.

"Virile Serial Opening Today at Ritz Here." *News-Journal.* Dec. 4, 1932, p. 12. Print.

"Young Chaney Would Make Own 'Name.'" *Fresno Morning Republican, The.* Feb. 13, 1932, p. 5. Print.

October 31, 1933

Beck, Calvin Thomas. *Heroes of the Horrors.* New York: Collier Books, 1975. Print.

"Chaney Widow's Life Ebbs." *Los Angeles Times, The.* October 15, 1933, p. 1. Print.

Gargiulo, Suzanne. *Lon Chaney's Shadow*. Bearmanor Media, 2009. Ebook.

Kingsley, Grace. "Husky Heroes Now in Vogue." *Los Angeles Times, The*. June 2, 1932, p. 32. Print.

Parsons, Louella. *Tampa Bay Times*. Jan. 27, 1933, p. 15. Print.

Pryor, Nancy. "Is Lon Chaney's Son Fated to Suffer for Films, Too?" *Movie Classic*. Jan. 1933, p. 54. Print.

Soanes, Wood. "Boyd and Young Chaney Hold Divergent Opinions on Utility of Doubles." *Oakland Tribune*. Feb. 26, 1933, p. 33. Print.

"Widow of Screen Star Inherited Bulk of His Estate." *Times Union*. Nov. 1, 1933, p. 20. Print.

June 25, 1936

Adams, George. "Today's Talk" (McNaught Syndicate). *Nashville Banner*. July 30, 1938, p. 12. Print.

"All-Time Film Rental Champs." *Variety*. Oct. 15, 1990.

Beck, Calvin Thomas. *Heroes of the Horrors*. New York: Collier Books, 1975. Print.

"Cash Given to Werners, Says Witness at Hearing." *Los Angeles Times, The*. June 18, 1936, p. 1. Print.

"Chaney Explains His Liquor Business Status." *Los Angeles Times, The*. June 7, 1936, p. 1. Print.

"Chaney, Jr., Reveals October 1st Wedding." *Fresno Bee, The*. Jan. 11, 1938, p. 16. Print.

"Chaney Ordered to Pay Support." *Los Angeles Times, The*. Dec. 20, 1938, p. 3. Print.

Gargiulo, Suzanne. *Lon Chaney's Shadow*. Bearmanor Media, 2009. Ebook.

"Guard Graft Witness as $500 Fixing Fee for 'Queen' Told." *Press Democrat, The*. June 18, 1936, p. 1. Print.

"Hollywood Report, The." *News-Democrat and Leader*. Jan. 3, 1935, p. 7. Print.

"Jesse James (1939)." *AFI Catalog of Feature Films*. www.catalog.afi.com. Web.

"Joy Parker Denies Part in Kidnaping." *San Francisco Examiner, The*. Sept. 20, 1934, p. 11. Print.

Laboratory playlets. *Napa Journal*. June 8, 1934, p. 2. Print.

"Lon Chaney, Jr. and Bride Admit Secret Marriage Last October." *Los Angeles Times, The*. Jan. 11, 1938, p. 21. Print.

"Lon Chaney, Jr.: Son of a Thousand Faces." *Biography*. Kevin Burns, Director. 1995.

"Lon Chaney, Jr. Weds." *Lincoln Star, The*. Jan. 10, 1938, p. 1. Print.

"Lon Chaney, Junior, Escapes Bad Injury." *Winnipeg Tribune, The*. Oct. 13, 1938, p. 11. Print.

"Lon Chaney Wealth Goal of Kidnapers." *Oakland Tribune*. July 28, 1934, p. 2. Print.

"Lon Chaney's Son Plans to Assume Name for Screen." *Indianapolis Star, The*. Jan. 5, 1935, p. 11. Print.

Mank, Gregory William. *It's Alive!* San Diego/New York: A.S. Barnes & Co., 1981. Print.

"Minister Acts for Marriage." *San Bernardino County Sun, The*. Jan. 12, 1938, p. 13. Print.

"Model Sues for Display of Picture." *Los Angeles Times, The*. Aug. 29, 1935, p. 28. Print.

"Mrs. Chaney Divorces Son of Late Thespian." *Los Angeles Times, The*. July 25, 1936, p. 4. Print.

"Must Pay Her." *Greenville News, The*. Dec. 21, 1938, p. 2. Print.

"Parkers Get Life Terms." *Los Angeles Times, The*. Oct. 6, 1934, p. 15. Print.

"Possibility of Parole Denied Convicted Trio." *News-Pilot*. Sept. 14, 1934, p. 1. Print.

"Puppy Litter Valued at $1,500." *Santa Rosa Republican*. April 12, 1934, p. 2. Print.

"'Queen Helen' Denies Promising Liquor Protection." *Pomona Progress Bulletin, The*. March 4, 1937, p. 1. Print.

Riley, Philip, ed. *The Wolf Man (The Original Shooting Script)*. Absecon, NJ: MagicImage Filmbooks, 1993. Print.

Smith, Don G. *Lon Chaney, Jr.: Horror Film Star*. Jefferson NC: McFarland and Company, 1996. Print.

"Son of Lon Chaney To Pay Alimony." *Pomona Progress Bulletin, The*. Dec. 20, 1938, p. 1. Print.

"Stardom of his father not his…" *Abilene Reporter-News*. Feb. 23, 1937, p. 6. Print.

Thomas, Bob. "Chaneys to Wed All Over Again." *Oakland Tribune*. Dec. 24, 1945, p. 7. Print.

"Weinblatt Strategy Assists Pair." *Wilmington Daily Press Journal*. March 6, 1937, p. 1. Print.

"Wife Seeking to Divorce Son of Lon Chaney." *Los Angeles Times, The*. June 26, 1936, p. 22. Print.

"Within the Rock." *Kingsport Times*. March 8, 1936, p. 10. Print.

"Woman Raps at Werners." *Los Angeles Times, The*. June 18, 1936, p. 6. Print.

"Young Lon Chaney's October Nuptials Are Admitted." *Appeal-Democrat*. Jan. 11, 1938, p. 2. Print.

"Young Chaney on Stand in $25,000 Suit for Damages." *San Francisco Examiner, The*. June 8, 1934, p. 5. Print.

October 27, 1941

Anger, Kenneth. *Hollywood Babylon II*. New York: Plume, 1984. Print.

Beck, Calvin Thomas. *Heroes of the Horrors*. New York: Collier Books, 1975. Print.

Brosnan, John. *Horror People, The*. New York: Plume, 1976. Print.

Brunas, Michael, John Brunas, and Tom Weaver. *Universal Horrors: The Studio's Classic Films, 1931-1946*. Jefferson NC: McFarland & Company Inc., 1990. Print.

"Chatter In Hollywood." *Sacramento Bee, The*. November 28, 1942, p. 15. Print.

"Creighton Chaney Says 'No.'" *Los Angeles Times, The*. August 9, 1932, p. 23. Print.

Everson, William K. *Classics of the Horror Film*. Secaucus, NJ: Citadel Press, 1974. Print.

Gourley, Jack and Gary Dorst. "A Man, A Myth, and Many Monsters." *Filmfax*. May 1990. Print.

Kiesling, Barrett C. "Lon Chaney Jr. Tells of Debt to Father." *Richmond Times-Dispatch*. May 25, 1941, p. 61. Print.

Lennig, Arthur. *Immortal Count, The*. Lexington: University Press of Kentucky, 2003. Print.

"Lon Chaney's Wagon 'Bug' Claim Settled." *Los Angeles Times*. November 17, 1944, p. 9. Print.

"Man Made Monster." *AFI Catalog of Feature Films*. www.catalog.afi.com. Web.

Mank, Gregory William. *It's Alive!* San Diego/New York: A.S. Barnes & Co., 1981. Print.

McClelland, Doug. *Golden Age of "B" Movies, The*. Bonanza Books, 1978. Print.

Monahan, Kaspar. "Shop Shows: Being a Joint Interview with Lon Chaney and Ruth Hussey." *Pittsburgh Press, The* (Pittsburgh, PA). March 15, 1943. Print.

"Of Mice and Men (1939)." *AFI Catalog of Feature Films*. www.catalog.afi.com. Web.

"One Million B.C." *AFI Catalog of Feature Films*. www.catalog.afi.com. Web.

"Orphaned Oddity." *Daily Press* (Newport News, VA). May 16, 1943, p. 21. Print.

Othman, Frederick C. "Werewolves Stalk Film Set Again." *Los Angeles Evening Citizen News*. November 22, 1941, p. 4. Print.

Parsons, Louella O. "Lon Chaney, Jr. Will Star in Steinbeck's Play, Cup of Gold." International News Service. *Sacramento Bee, The*. Dec. 19, 1939, p. 18. Print.

"Recipes the Whole Family Will Enjoy." *Mogen David Wine Cookbook*, c. 1947. Print.

Riley, Philip, ed. *The Wolf Man (The Original Shooting Script)*. Absecon, NJ: MagicImage Filmbooks, 1993. Print.

Siodmak, Curt. *Wolf Man's Maker*. Folkestone, England: Scarecrow Press, 1997. Print.

Smith, Don G. *Lon Chaney, Jr.: Horror Film Star*. Jefferson NC: McFarland and Company, 1996. Print.

Steinbeck, Elaine and Robert Wallsten, eds. *Steinbeck: A Life in Letters*. Penguin Books, 1976.

Svehla, Gary J. and Susan, eds. *Lon Chaney, Jr.* Baltimore: Midnight Marquee Press, 1997. Print.

United Press. "Lon Chaney Jr. Turns Down Dad's Film Role." *Dispatch, The*. May 1, 1952, p. 28. Print.

August 17, 1944

"Actor Lon Chaney Jr.'s home…" *Daily News*. March 31, 1945, p. 3. Print.

"Actor, 'Pool,' and Problem." *Valley Times*. January 15, 1947, p. 3. Print.

"America's Miracle: Free Enterprise in Action in Southern California—General Water Heater Corp." *Los Angeles Times, The* (Los Angeles, CA). March 20, 1956, p. 14. Print.

"Assorted Monsters Prove Unusual Guests at Party." *Los Angeles Evening Citizen News*. April 27, 1944, p. 16. Print.

Beck, Calvin Thomas. *Heroes of the Horrors*. New York: Collier Books, 1975. Print.

"Boy May Adopt Lon Chaneys as His Parents." *Los Angeles Times, The*. August 17, 1944, p. 13. Print.

"Brother of Adopted Son of Movie Star in City." *Bakersfield Californian, The*. August 25, 1944, p. 9. Print.

Carroll, Harrison. "Behind the Scenes Hollywood." *Press Democrat, The*. March 12, 1944, p. 14. Print.

Carroll, Harrison. "Behind the Scenes Hollywood." *Press Democrat, The*. April 19, 1944, p. 12. Print.

Carroll, Harrison. "Behind the Scenes Hollywood." *Press Democrat, The*. December 6, 1944, p. 14. Print.

Carroll, Harrison. "Behind the Scenes Hollywood." *Press Democrat, The*. December 28, 1944, p. 10. Print.

Carroll, Harrison. "Behind the Scenes Hollywood." *Press Democrat, The*. February 21, 1945, p. 10. Print

Carroll, Harrison. "Behind the Scenes Hollywood." *Press Democrat, The*. October 4, 1945, p. 16. Print.

Carroll, Harrison. "Behind the Scenes Hollywood." *Press Democrat, The*. October 26, 1945, p. 12. Print.

Carroll, Harrison. "Behind the Scenes Hollywood." *Press Democrat, The*. November 2, 1945, p. 14. Print.

Carroll, Harrison. "Behind the Scenes Hollywood." *Santa Rosa Republican, The*. January 25, 1946, p. 14. Print.

Churchill, Reba and Bonnie. "Hollywood Diary." *Valley Times*. February 22, 1947, p. 15. Print.

Coons, Robbin. "Robbin Coons in Hollywood." Monrovia News-Post. September 5, 1944, p. 8. Print.

D'avila, Robert D. "Obituary: Classic clothier known for his local knowledge." *Sacramento Bee, The*. November 30, 2007, p. B3. Print.

"Deaths." *Los Angeles Times, The*. August 19, 1943, p. 29. Print.

"Deaths." *Metropolitan Pasadena Star-News*. November 18, 1946, p. 5.

"Figure in '33 Kidnaping Found Dead." *Los Angeles Times, The*. May 12, 1944, p. 15. Print.

"Frankenstein Meets the Wolf Man." Press book. Issued by Universal Studios, 1943. Print.

"From Malibu Beach to the motion picture studios…" *Los Angeles Evening Citizen News*. November 13, 1944, p. 14. Print.

Gourley, Jack and Gary Dorst. "A Man, A Myth, and Many Monsters." *Filmfax*. May 1990. Print.

Hopper, Hedda. "Looking at Hollywood." *Los Angeles Times*. July 27, 1944, p. 10. Print.

"House of Frankenstein." *AFI Catalog*. www.catalog.afi.com. Web.

"Incinerator Starts Fire." *Los Angeles Times*. March 31, 1945, p. 9.

"Hunt Chaney Kin." *Los Angeles Evening Citizen News*. December 1, 1945, p. 1. Print.

"It's Up to the Boy." *Press and Sun-Bulletin* (Binghamton, NY). August 18, 1944, p. 24. Print.

Johnson, Erskine. "Bad Luck Comes to a Sound Stage." *Daily News*. November 23, 1942, p. 21. Print.

Lennig, Arthur. *Immortal Count, The*. Lexington: University Press of Kentucky, 2003. Print.

"Lon Chaney Battling Swimming Pool Deal." *Los Angeles Times*. January 10, 1947, p. 13. Print.

"Lon Chaney Denies Owing Hospital Bill." *Sacramento Bee*. February 4, 1947, p. 8. Print.

"Lon Chaney, Jr., Buys Ranch in El Dorado." *Sacramento Bee, The*. April 26, 1944, p. 11. Print.

"Lon Chaney, Jr., May Legalize Adoption of Stockton Youngster." *Sacramento Bee, The*. August 18, 1944, p. 9. Print.

"Lon Chaney Plans 'Copter Service to Malibu Beach." *San Fernando Valley Times*. November 6, 1944, p. 25. Print.

"Lon Chaney's Cousin Object of Search." *La Crosse Tribune*. December 1, 1945, p. 2. Print.

"Lon Chaneys Plan to Adopt 8-Year-Old." *Los Angeles Evening Citizen News*. August 17, 1944, p. 13. Print.

MacPherson, Virginia. "Hollywood Film Shop." *Chico Record*. April 18, 1944, p. 2. Print.

Mank, Gregory William. *It's Alive!* San Diego/New York: A.S. Barnes & Co., 1981. Print.

Manners, Dorothy. "Hollywood In Shorts." *San Francisco Examiner, The*. November 1, 1944, p. 11. Print.

Manners, Dorothy. "The Birds and the Bees to Star Tiny Jane Powell." *San Francisco Examiner*. August 13, 1946, p. 10. Print.

MacPherson, Virginia. "Horror Monster Dracula, Wolf Man in Thriller." *Hanford Sentinel*. October 8, 1945, p. 3. Print.

McClelland, Doug. *Golden Age of "B" Movies, The.* Bonanza Books, 1978. Print.

McCullough, Laura. "From the Set...Janet Ann Gallow." *Operator 13 Productions.* March 26, 2012. Web.

Millier, Arthur. "Lon Seeks New Roles as Monster." *Los Angeles Times.* November 4, 1945, p. 25. Print.

"Missing Man Sends for Clothing." *La Crosse Tribune.* December 12, 1945, p. 5. Print.

Monahan, Kaspar. "Being a Joint Interview with Lon Chaney and Ruth Hussey." *Pittsburgh Press, The.* March 15, 1943, p. 8. Print.

"Monsterpalooza 2015: Janet Ann Gallow Interview." *Nerd Soapbox, The.* April 3, 2015. YouTube. Web.

Mosby, Aline. "Movies' Bad Men Team Up at Last." *Los Angeles Evening Citizen News.* September 1, 1947, p. 10. Print.

"Movie Star Is Sued by El Dorado Retailers." *Sacramento Bee.* February 7, 1946, p. 12.

"Orphaned Oddity." *Daily Press* (Newport News, VA). May 16, 1943, p. 21. Print.

Othman, Frederick C. "Hollywood Film Shop." *Chico Record.* October 25, 1942, p. 2. Print.

Parsons, Louella. "Lon Chaney, Jr., Will Get New Start in Career as Comedian." *Sacramento Bee.* June 21, 1946, p. 14. Print.

Peary, Danny, ed. *Close-Ups.* New York: Simon and Shuster, 1978. Print.

"Police Raid Lon Chaney Disc Session." *San Fernando Valley Times.* March 26, 1945, p. 24. Print.

Schallert, Edwin. "Big Town Show to Become Movie." *Los Angeles Times.* October 22, 1945, p. 9. Print.

Sloan, Lloyd L. "A Few Leftover Notes at the End of a Week." *Los Angeles Evening Citizen News*. May 10, 1947, p. 6. Print.

Smith, Don G. *Lon Chaney, Jr.: Horror Film Star, 1906-1973*. Jefferson, NC: MacFarland & Company, 1996. Print.

Thomas, Bob. "Hollywood." *The Times*. October 10, 1945, p. 8. Print.

Thomas, Bob. "Chaneys to Wed All Over Again." *Oakland Tribune*. December 24, 1945, p. 7. Print.

Thomas, Bob. "Lon Chaney Scared by Boogie Men*!*" *Los Angeles Evening Citizen News*. February 1, 1947, p. 4. Print.

Thomas, Bob. "Only 36 Films Now Before the Lenses." *Los Angeles Evening Citizen News*. August 9, 1946, p. 4. Print.

Thomas, Bob. "Press Agent Acts in Own Picture." *Los Angeles Evening Citizen News*. December 4, 1945, p. 6. Print.

"Violation Charge Halts Work on Lon Chaney Pool." *Daily News*. January 9, 1947, p. 8. Print.

February 5, 1948

"Abbott and Costello Meet Frankenstein File, The. Part 1." Abbott and Costello Quarterly, #53. 2008. Print.

"Abbott and Costello Meet Frankenstein File, The. Part 4." Abbott and Costello Quarterly, #56. 2008. Print.

Brunas, Michael, John Brunas, and Tom Weaver. *Universal Horrors: The Studio's Classic Films, 1931-*

1946. Jefferson NC: McFarland & Company Inc., 1990. Print.

"Bud Abbott Lou Costello Meet Frankenstein." *AFI Catalog*. www.afi.com. Web.

Churchill, Reba and Bonnie. "Hollywood Diary." *Valley Times*. Feb. 21, 1948, p. 13. Print.

"Freeway Free-For-All Jams Cars for Blocks." *Los Angeles Times, The*. March 3, 1948, p. 2. Print.

Gargiulo, Suzanne. *Lon Chaney's Shadow*. Bearmanor Media, 2009. Ebook.

Gourley, Jack and Gary Dorst. "A Man, A Myth, and Many Monsters." *Filmfax*. May 1990. Print.

"He Ruled a Raw Frontier." *San Francisco Examiner, The*. Feb. 15, 1948, p. 26. Print.

Hopper, Hedda. "Looking at Hollywood." *Los Angeles Times, The*. Jan. 10, 1948, p. 7. Print.

Lennig, Arthur. *The Immortal Count*. University Press of Kentucky, 2003. Print.

Johnson, Erskine. "Bing Isn't Bothered About Little Things Like Toupees." *Ventura County Star-Free Press*. June 8, 1948, p. 8. Print.

"Juniors Make Good in Own Film Careers." *Oakland Tribune*. March 18, 1948, p. 30. Print.

K.W. "Lobero Theatre Summer Season of Plays Termed 'Outstanding'." *Lompoc Record*. July 22, 1948, p. 5. Print.

"Lenore Aubert Joins Dracula Entourage." *Los Angeles Times, The*. Jan. 26, 1948, p. 11. Print.

Lompoc Record. July 8, 1948, p. 8. Print.

Mallory, Michael. *Universal Studios Monsters: A Legacy of Horror*. New York: Universe Publishing, 2009. Print.

Mank, Gregory William. *It's Alive*. San Diego/New York: A.S. Barnes & Company, Inc, 1941.

McCelland, Doug. *Golden Age of B Movies, The*. Bonanza Books, 1978. Print.

Mulholland, Jim. *Abbott and Costello Book, The*. New York: Warner Books, 1975. Print.

Othman, Frederick C. "Hollywood Film Shop." *Chico Record*. October 25, 1942, p. 2. Print.

Riley, Philip J., ed. *Abbott and Costello Meet Frankenstein: The Original Shooting Script*. Absecon, NJ: MagicImage Filmbooks, 1990. Print.

Scott, John L. "Five Summer Houses Will Open This Month." *Los Angeles Times*. June 13, 1948, p. 49. Print.

Schallert, Edwin. "Film and Drama." *Los Angeles Times*. March 26, 1948, p. 15. Print.

Smith, Don G. Lon Chaney, Jr.: Horror Film Star, 1906-1973. Jefferson, NC: MacFarland & Company, 1996. Print.

Soanes, Wood. "Three Openings a Puzzle for Bay Area First Nighters." *Oakland Tribune*. May 31, 1948, p. 14. Print.

"Son of Actor Lon Chaney Being Held." *Wilmington Daily Press Journal*. March 3, 1948, p. 10. Print.

"Steinbeck Play at Lobero Theater." *Santa Maria Times*. July 12, 1948, p. 5. Print.

Thomas, Bob. *Bud & Lou*. Philadelphia/New York: J.B. Lippincott Company, 1977. Print.

Thomas, Bob. "Hollywood." *News-Pilot.* March 3, 1948, p. 2. Print.

Thomas, Bob. "Hollywood." *Johnson City Press,* March 5, 1948, p. 5. Print.

"Tradition of Chills and Thrills." *San Francisco Examiner, The.* Aug. 2, 1948, p. 11. Print.

"Two Held After Fight on Cahuenga Freeway." *Valley Times.* March 3, 1948, p. 1. Print.

"Weatherman Offers Hope for Downpour. *Los Angeles Times, The.* Feb. 5, 1948, p. 1. Print.

Epilogue

"Arrested on Theft Charge." *Colton Carrier.* June 16, 1949, p. 4. Print.

Beck, Calvin Thomas. *Heroes of the Horrors.* New York: Collier Books, 1975. Print.

Blake, Michael F. *A Thousand Faces.* Lanham/New York/Oxford: Vestal Press, 1995. Ebook.

Blake, Michael F. *Lon Chaney: The Man Behind the Thousand Faces.* Lanham, MD: The Vestal Press, 1990. Print.

"Chaney's Grandson Jailed for Theft." *Johnson City Press.* June 16, 1949, p. 19. Print.

"Chaney's Widow Dies at Age 78." *San Bernardino County Sun.* November 23, 1967, p. 16. Print.

"Fallbrook Activist Killed in Accident." *North County Times.* May 7, 1992, p. 13. Print.

"Former Huronian Weds Lon Chaney." *The Daily Plainsman.* December 12, 1948, p. 6. Print.

Gourley, Jack and Gary Dorst. "A Man, A Myth, and Many Monsters." *Filmfax*. May 1990. Print.

"Grandson of Lon Chaney Held in Memphis Theft." *Knoxville News Sentinel*. June 16, 1949, p. 38. Print.

"Held in Hotel Theft." *Minneapolis Star*. June 17, 1949, p. 4. Print.

"Hostess Forfeits Bond in Arrest." *Los Angeles Times*. May 12, 1949, p. 20. Print.

"Jailed Gob Says He's Actor's Son." *Long Beach Independent*. June 16, 1949, p. 3. Print.

"Lon Chaney, Jr.: Son of a Thousand Faces." *Biography*. Kevin Burns, Director. 1995.

Peary, Danny, ed. *Close-Ups*. New York: Simon and Shuster, 1978. Print.

Smith, Don G. *Lon Chaney, Jr.: Horror Film Star, 1906-1973*. Jefferson, NC: MacFarland & Company, 1996. Print.

Acknowledgements

Dick, Bernard F. *City of Dreams*. Lexington: University of Kentucky Press, 1997. Print.

Index

Abbott and Costello Meet Frankenstein (film). 4, 7, 162, 183*n*, 185*n*.

Abbott, Bud. 71, 137-140, 143-146, 148-149, 151-152, 162, 182*n*.

Ankers, Evelyn. 71, 83, 87, 94-95, 97, 98-100, 102-103, 110, 120-121, 139, 146, 178*n*.

Atwill, Lionel. 83, 110, 164, 177*n*.

Barton, Charles. 143-144, 146-147, 149.

Brain of Frankenstein, The (working title). 4, 136, 138, 139.

Bush, Stella (*half-sister*). 37.

Bush, William (*step-father*). 23, 37, 135.

Carradine, John. 126, 127, 130.

Chaney, Cleva Creighton (*mother*). 9-21, 23, 25, 26, 34-37, 46, 52, 54, 157, 168*n*, 169*n*, 171*n*, 181*n*, 184*n*.

Chaney, Creighton (Lon Jr.).

    Affairs: 46, 54, 55, 66, 155, 172*n*, 179*n*.

    Alleged spousal abuse: 174*n*.

    Attempted suicide: 1, 5-7, 25, 150, 152, 155, 158, 165, 166.

    Birth: 2, 13, 169*n*.

    Death: 160.

    Divorce: 54-55, 62, 64, 174*n*.

    Drinking: 3, 4, 52, 66, 68, 86-87, 95, 111, 118-121, 128, 130, 146, 159, 174*n*, 183*n*.

    Physical description: 24, 25, 29, 44, 48, 68, 76, 121, 169*n*, 170*n*, 180*n*.

Chaney, Dorothy Hinckley (*first wife*). 2, 28-31, 35, 39-40, 54, 55, 62, 64, 70, 150, 172*n*, 175*n*, 183*n*.

Chaney, Hazel Hastings (*step-mother*). 14, 22-23, 29, 32-34, 35-36, 38, 41, 44, 46, 47, 49-53, 56, 57, 142, 169*n*, 173*n*.

Chaney, Leonidis F. "Lon" (*father*).
> *Birth*: 10.
> *Death*: 2, 32-34.
> *Divorce*: 17-19, 21, 34.
> *Father to Creighton*: 23, 25, 26, 60, 155, 156.
> *Lying about Cleva's death*: 21, 36-37, 156.

Chaney, Lon Ralph (*son*). 5, 30, 45, 54, 123, 132, 156, 169*n*, 179*n*, 184*n*.

Chaney, Patsy Beck (*second wife*). 1, 3, 5-6, 16, 62, 65-66, 73, 74, 76, 85-86, 107-108, 110, 129, 132, 133, 135, 150, 157, 174*n*, 175*n*, 176*n*, 178*n*, 181*n*, 186*n*.

Chaney, Ronald Creighton (*son*). 1-2, 30, 54, 123, 149-150, 179*n*, 181*n*, 183-184*n*.

Chaney, Ronald Curt (*grandson*). 64, 159, 184*n*.

Costello, Lou. 71, 137-141, 143-146, 148, 149, 152, 182*n*.

Crawford, Broderick. 71, 73-74, 86-87, 99, 118, 123, 153, 176*n*.

Cregar, Laird. 158, 177*n*.

Denning, Richard. 120-121, 180*n*.

Devine, Andy. 118, 133.

Devine, Burrell Lee Howard. 107-108, 112, 179*n*.

Frankenstein Meets the Wolf Man (*film*). 113-117, 141, 162, 171*n*, 180*n*.

Gallow, Janet Ann. 110.
Ghost of Frankenstein (film). 109-110, 116.
House of Dracula (film). 130-132, 140.
House of Frankenstein (film). 125-127, 130, 174*n*.
Jeske, John. 27-28, 30, 32, 33, 35, 40, 44, 50-53, 55-58, 129, 142, 173*n*.
Karloff, Boris. 82, 83, 84, 85, 88, 109, 110, 120, 125, 126, 127, 152, 164, 179*n*, 181*n*.
Kenton, Erle C. 110, 125, 130.
LeBorg, Reginald. 111, 118, 124-125, 159, 160.
Lennie's Ranch (*property in Cool, CA*). 128, 129, 132, 135, 180*n*.
Lon Chaney, Jr. Café (*business*). 60-61, 62-64.
Lugosi, Bela. 82, 94, 100, 110, 112, 114, 115, 116, 117, 120, 126, 141, 142-143, 144-145, 146, 147-148, 152, 164, 178*n*, 179*n*, 180*n*, 182*n*, 183*n*.
MacPherson, Virginia. 125, 126, 130.
Man Made Monster (film). 82-85, 88, 99, 169*n*.
Massey, Ilona. 115, 116, 180*n*.
Meredith, Burgess. 75, 77, 78.
Milestone, Lewis. 75-77, 78.
Moose (*Chaney's dog*). 101, 114, 115, 123.
Neill, Roy William. 113-114, 116.
Of Mice and Men (film). 3, 75-80, 88, 153, 158, 163, 169*n*, 176*n*.
Parsons, Louella. 41, 43, 47, 79, 134.
Pierce, Jack P. 83-84, 94, 95-96, 97, 105, 109, 110, 125, 126, 137, 146.
Rains, Claude. 93, 94, 102-103, 112, 170*n*, 181*n*.

Randolph, Jane. 141, 145, 149.

Salkow, Lester. 5-6, 168*n*.

Siodmak, Curt. 88-90, 92, 93, 96, 98, 113, 117, 125, 136, 156, 169*n*, 178*n*.

Steinbeck, John. 3, 73, 75, 77, 78, 79, 80, 152.

Strange, Glenn. 126-127, 130, 141, 145, 146-147.

Verdugo, Elena. 125, 127-128, 174*n*.

Waggner, George. 82-84, 93, 94, 97, 99, 101-102, 116, 117.

Wolf Man, The (film). 3, 71-72, 85, 88-106, 107, 109, 112, 113, 115, 116, 136, 138, 158, 163, 164, 165, 169*n*, 170*n*, 178*n*, 179*n*.

Woodmansee, Barry. 6-7, 142, 168*n*.

Zucco, George. 120, 126.

Printed in Great Britain
by Amazon